INTERNATIONAL ENTREPRENEURSHIP AND LEGITIMACY

A Study of Chinese International Firms

国际企业家精神与合法化

基于中国国际企业的研究

YANG Hairu

杨海儒　著

上海三联书店

ABSTRACT

This study aims to explore what is the motivation of international entrepreneurship in the domestic market and how international entrepreneurial firms survive in foreign market. Based on a sample of 212 Chinese international firms, it examines the internationalization of organizational field as an antecedent of international entrepreneurship from a neoinstitutional theory perspective. Exploitative and exploratory learning are considered as consequences of international entrepreneurship, because firms seek to achieve legitimacy in the host country. The nonlinear relationship between exploitative and exploratory learning and performance are further tested. Findings suggest that isomorphic pressure from the organizational field will cause firms to engage in international entrepreneurial activities. In order to get legitimacy in a host country, international entrepreneurship, in turn, is positively associated with the above two learning processes. Results also support that although exploitative and exploratory learning are beneficial, they would weaken a firm's performance in a foreign market, after a certain point.

Keywords: international entrepreneurship, institutional isomorphism, neoinstitutional theory, legitimacy

致 谢

此书能出版首先感谢我的博士生导师香港城市大学 Daniel Ding 教授，他不仅仅是我学习上的导师，更是我生命转折的恩人。近四年的接触他的宽容和鼓励，才能够让我这样一个资质一般的人获得博士学位。我的学习、工作、生活很多都受到了恩惠。

还要感谢我的家人，尽最大努力给我创造时间让我工作、研究。我那一双儿女虽然工作中给我带来的是麻烦，是时间的占用，可是给我带来的快乐是难以取代的。而且做好榜样的动力也一直激励着我要尽我能努力向前，做好工作。感谢我多年的同事，在工作中的帮忙和相助。虽然是同事，但是我们的相处和亲人又有什么差异呢？

感谢上海金融学院、国家自然科学基金项目：私募股权投资机制下企业家精神的研究：结构化视角（编号：71102001）、教育部人文社会科学研究项目：制度环境对我国企业国际企业家精神的影响机制研究(编号:10YJC630323),上海市教委科研创新项目对出版的支持。

杨海儒

2015 年 5 月 13 日

TABLE OF CONTENTS

List of Table

List of Figure

Chapter 1
Introduction

This chapter lays the foundation for this study. After a brief review of the international entrepreneurship, research gaps will be identified. Two research questions and the theoretical model will be proposed. I will also explain why the research was carried out in China. Research methods including data collection and analysis method and the outline of this study are presented.

1.1 International Entrepreneurship — a Brief Review

With the globalization of the world economy, international entrepreneurship has received more attention over the past decade (Brush 1993, 1995; Hitt & Bartkus, 1997; Hisrich et al. , 1996; Zahra & George 2002). Particularly, in China, the biggest emerging market, with its "Open Door" policies after 1978 and accession to the Word Trade Organization (WTO) in 2001, its integration with the global economy has been at an accelerated pace. Currently, internationalization is of paramount importance to Chinese firms.

Extant research in international entrepreneurship explores the organizational factors such as top management team's characteristics (Bloodgood, Sapienza & Almeida, 1996; McDougall & Oviatt, 1996; Oviatt & McDougall, 1995), and firm resources (Oviatt & McDougall, 1995) as antecedents of international entrepreneurship. There have also been investigations into the influence of strategic factors such as generic strategy (McDougall, 1989; Oviatt & McDougall, 1995) and functional strategy (Bloodgood, Sapienza & Almeida, 1996; McDougall, 1989) on international entrepreneurship. However, these studies focus only on the technical and organizational level without mentioning institutional level (Parsons, 1960; Petit, 1960).

Organizations are in an open system instead of a closed-system (Petit, 1960). They have to survive in their institutional environment and attempt to secure legitimacy (Tompson, 1967). According to neoinstitutional theory, organization behaviors are influenced by institutional environment (Dimaggio & Powell, 1983). Particularly, in recent internationalization studies, interest in the institutional environment has increased rapidly (Child & Rodrigues, 2005; Dunning, 2006; Meyer & Nguyen, 2005; Cross, Liu & Zheng, 2007; Peng, 2002; Wright et al., 2005; Yiu, Lau & Bruton, 2007). However, despite the valuable contributions of these works, they treat institutional environment as the usual market environment and few studies have explored it from the institutional isomorphism perspective.

This study attempts to fill this important gap in the literature. Building on neoinstitutional theory, this study investigates the antecedents for firms to take international entrepreneurial activities in the domestic market and how international entrepreneurial firms survive in foreign markets.

1.2 Research Questions

The objectives of this study are to investigate two research questions:

(1) In the domestic market, what is the antecedent for firms to take international entrepreneurial activities?

(2) After going abroad, how do international entrepreneurial firms survive in foreign markets?

This study adopts the neoinstitutional theory to explain why firms choose to take international entrepreneurial activities and how these firms survive in foreign market.

According to neoinstitutional theory, organizations face the pressure of "institutional isomorphism" to conform to rules and norms, strategies and processes deemed legitimacy by its external environment (DiMaggio & Powell, 1983). A firm in its organizational field faces this pressure to conform to certain norms, since violating them may lead to the legitimacy problems and thus affects its ability to secure resources and social support (DiMaggio & Powell, 1983; Powell & DiMaggio, 1991; Tolbert& Zucker, 1983). After joining the WTO, the social expectation for internationalization is stronger and China is more eager to integrate into the global environment. According to neoinstitutional theory, organizations will be awarded for being similar to other organizations in their fields. The similarity can make firms easier to transact with other organizations, to attract career-minded staff etc. (DiMaggio & Powell, 1983; Powell & DiMaggio 1991). Currently, with market growth of foreign competitors in China, domestic competitors, suppliers and customers going abroad, some organizational fields in China are being more international. With the organizational field expanding geographically, isomorphism pressure of internationalization has commenced. Thus, the increasingly internationalization of their organizational fields provides firms with legitimacy to take international entrepreneurship activities.

Before firms go abroad, the isomorphic pressure in the domestic market pushes firms to demonstrate international entrepreneurship. However, after firms go abroad, the legitimacy pressure from a host country dominates the firms' behavior. In order to get legitimacy and compete with local firms, firms have to devote themselves to learning activities to acquire host country spccific knowlcdgc which influcnccs a firm's ability to adapt its product to local market conditions. Therefore, international firms' intrinsic disadvantages that are due to a lack of legitimacy can be substantially overcome. Meanwhile, from a subjective perspective, international entrepreneurial firms also provide the learning culture for acquiring host country knowledge. That is a firm with international entrepreneurial orientation establishes relative rules and norms for expanding efforts toward supporting learning activities to acquire foreign market knowledge.

Consistent with March (1991) model, organizational

learning can be classified into exploitative learning and exploratory learning. Considering that maintaining adaptiveness requires both exploiting existing competencies and exploring new ones (Floyd & Lane, 2000), firms with international entrepreneurial orientation will carry out these two kinds of learning activities to acquire host country knowledge.

Figure 1.1 illustrates the conceptual framework proposed by this study. The framework shows that in order to get legitimacy in the domestic market, the internationalization of an organizational field forces a firm to take international entrepreneurial activities. When firms go abroad, in order to get legitimacy in foreign market, firms have to get foreign market knowledge through exploitative and exploratory learning to improve their performance.

1.3 Research Settings

This study was conducted within a context of the transitional economy in China. In selecting China as the focus of the study, the following factors were particularly considered:

1. As Shenkar and von Glinow (1994) pointed out, China is an ideal site for testing the generalizability of Western

organizational and management theories. China has a population distinct culture and political system, and strong economy; International entrepreneurship theory should be explored within such an environment so that implications can expand knowledge about international entrepreneurship. Thus, China was selected as the research setting, which could enrich the understanding of the nature of international entrepreneurship and contribute to the generalizability of the existing body of research.

2. In China, the regulatory environment is under reform and become more supportive for firms to "go out". China has been developing from a centrally planned to a market-based economy since the "open-door policy" was promulgated in 1978. During the reform, the Chinese government took effective measures including removing regulatory barriers and establishing new legal regulations to foster internationalization. From 1978 – 1985, the beginning of Chinese economic reform, the internationalization step was slow because investing abroad was strictly restrained. Only some state-owned trading corporations were allowed to invest abroad. In 1985 the promulgated regulations relating to the procedure and management of establishing non-trade joint ventures in foreign countries begin to abolish some regulatory barriers and simplify administrative

procedures. The Chinese government intended to establish certain policies to encourage internationalization. In 1992, a milestone event occurred in China. That is, Deng Xiaoping's journey to the South. Deng Xiaoping's journey to the South had brought Chinese internationalization to a new stage. In 1998, the "go out" strategy was formalized in the 10th five-year plan. Moreover, in 2001, China was accepted as a member of the World Trade Organization (WTO). After joining the WTO, China was more eager to integrate into the global environment. With the furious domestic competitive pressures and the opening of once protected markets, in the 11th five-year plan the Chinese government emphasized again the necessity of "go out" for Chinese firms and Chinese economic development. Key events in the evaluation of China's internationalization approval process are presented in Table1. 1.

The fundamental changes in China's economic transition from a planned economy to a market economy pose severe challenges for firms in terms of internationalization. Thus, China provides a fascinating ground for testing and refining the boundaries of existing theories and developing new ones (Peng & Health, 1996). However, up to now, these have been very limited to knowledge about international entrepreneurship, let alone empirical evidence about the institutional environment influence on international entrepreneurship. This study can bridge this gap, and stimulate more international entrepreneurship research in transitional economies.

3. The regulatory environment of an emerging economy can determine the will of a firm to internationalize (Buckley et al. 2007). A straightforward, liberal policy towards internationalization could encourage internationalization, while regulatory barriers for internationalization will lead to constrained internationalization. As mentioned above, the political and economic climate in China is increasingly supportive for firms' internationalization.

Unlike the regulatory environment, which can change readily, the cognitive environment is quite resilient. It is often socially constructed over time and comes to be "perceived as an objective and external to the actors: not as man-made but a natural and factual order" (Scott, 1995). According to the definition provided by Busenitz et al., (2000), the cognitive environment consists of the knowledge and skills possessed by the people in a country pertaining to establishing and operating an international firm. At the beginning of economic reform in China, people did not even know how to establish a new business.

Let alone talk about how to identify international opportunities. However, countries' regulations and governments tend to affect cognitive dimension (Busenitz, 2000). With the development of regulative environment, more people possess knowledge about internationalization.

The normative environment is well-accepted, as well as non-statutory authority systems that guide the actions of organizations and individuals (Scott, 1995). According to the definition provided by Busenitz et al., (2000), the normative environment refers to the degree to which a country's residents admire and value international activities. At the beginning of reform, most Chinese people reject to accept reform and take it as society degradation. However, with the development of economic reform, Chinese people value and admire international activities. The Chinese institutional environment is changing rapidly and get more supportive for firm internationalization. Thus, research on Chinese firms' internationalization needs be conducted.

In summary, the supportive "go out" policy, the rapid export growth of Chinese firms and the increasing numbers of foreign firms coming into China have made China an ideal setting for studying international entrepreneurship. China is on its way to internationalization and more Chinese firms would like to choose to compete in the international market. Thus, this study offers the possibility of insights into international entrepreneurship in an increasingly open economy.

1.4 Research Methodology

A flow chart of the methodological process is shown in Figure 1.1. The research involves the examination of the relationships among the internationalization of organizational field, international entrepreneurship, exploitative and exploratory learning and performance.

First, a questionnaire was developed on the basis of an extensive literature review. Previous studies on institutional environment, organizational learning and international entrepreneurship were the basis for developing the questionnaire. Most of the measurement scales are from Western studies. In order to ensure the measurement scales retained their psychometric properties when employed in China, structured interviews were conducted. After developing the questionnaire, a pretest study was carried out. In this study, multiple-items measures were developed for all the constructs. Therefore, all dimensions were confirmed by using confirmatory factor analysis. Third, the antecedent effect of organizational field on international entrepreneurship was tested by using multiple regression analysis. Fourth, to test the mediation effect, I followed the regression procedures suggested by Baron and Kenny (1986). Finally, multiple regression analysis was adopted to test the inverted U-shape.

1.5 Outline of the Study

This study is organized into six chapters to examine the above mentioned research questions.

- Chapter One, the current chapter, provides a general overview of the study.
- Chapter Two, starting with the literature review on the theory of internationalization, I present the theoretical perspectives, models, key concepts and empirical findings in the international entrepreneurship literature. By reviewing the international entrepreneurship theory, relative definition and research streams in international entrepreneurship, the second chapter provides the foundation for exploring the relationship between organizational field, international entrepreneurship and organization learning.

• Chapter Three presents the theoretical framework and discusses the research hypotheses addressed in this study.

• Chapter Four describes the methodology, including such aspects as sampling, measurement and data analysis methods employed in this study.

• Chapter Five, the results of hypotheses testing are provided without drawing any general implications.

• Chapter Six summarizes discussions and conclusions of this research. The contributions, research implications, limitations and directions for further research are also included. Figure 1.2 presents the structure of this study.

1.6 Chapter Summary

This chapter lays the foundation for the study. Firstly, it has a brief review of international entrepreneurship. This is followed by proposing the research questions of this study. Research settings and research methodology are also presented. Finally the outline of the study is presented. On these foundations, the study proceeds with a detailed description of the research.

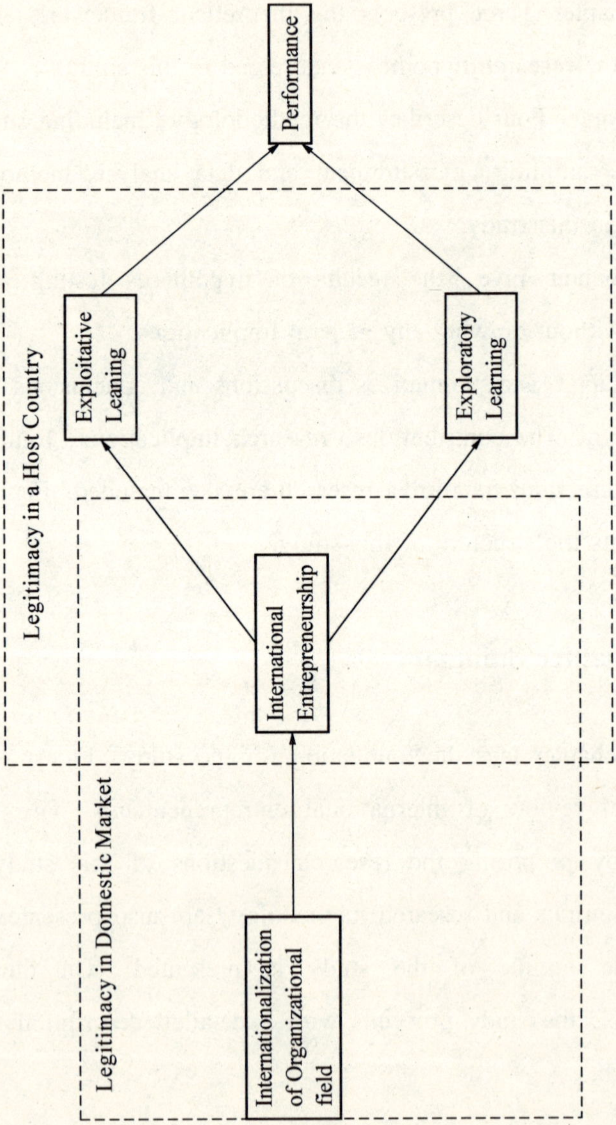

Figure 1.1 Research Framework

Table 1.1 Key stages in Chinese policy development

Time	Event
1979 - 1985	The beginning of "open door policy"
1985 - 1991	In 1985, Chinese government abolished restrictive policies and allowed more enterprise to invest abroad.
1992 - 1998	In 1992, Deng Xiaoping's journey to the South had brought Chinese internationalization to a new stage.
1998 - 2001	In 1998, "go out" strategy is firstly formalized in the 10th five-year plan.
Since 2001	In 2001, China was accepted as a member of word trade organization (WTO). In 11th five-year plan Chinese government emphasized again the necessity of "go out" for Chinese firms and Chinese economy development.

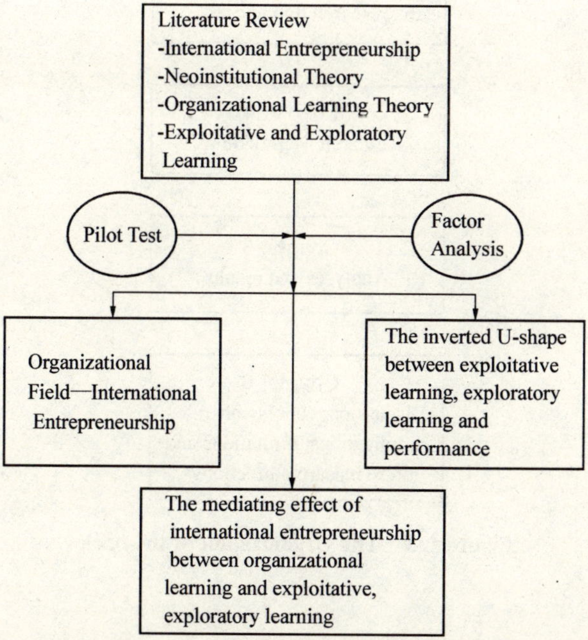

Figure 1.2 Research Process Flowchart

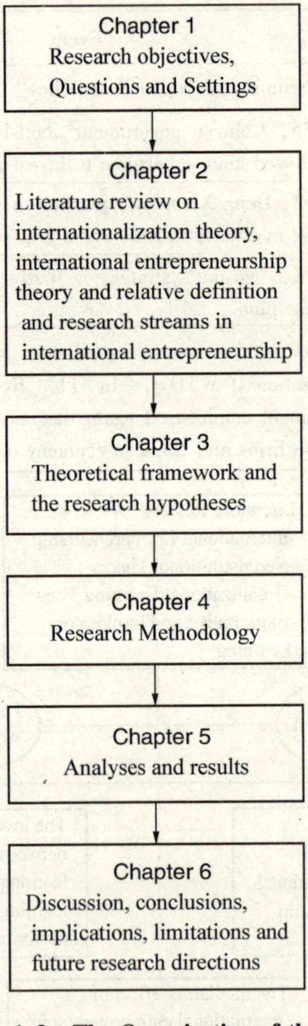

Figure 1.3 The Organization of the book

Chapter 2
Literature Review

This chapter presents the theoretical perspectives, models, key concepts and empirical findings in the international entrepreneurship literature. The objective is to review the foundations in the literature and research in the field of international entrepreneurship and to see what the determinants of international entrepreneurship are. The chapter is divided into four sections. First, the internationalization theories are reviewed. Then, with the theory development, the international entrepreneurship theory and relative definitions are reviewed. After that, I concentrate on reviewing the literature relevant to the research streams on the determinants of international entrepreneurship. Finally, a brief summary is presented.

2.1 Literature Review of International Entrepreneurship Theory

2.1.1 Uppsala Internationalization Theory

According to Anderson's (2000) classification of international business, there are mainly two approaches to explain internationalization: the economic view and the process view. The economic view focuses on explaining *why* internationalization takes place. In contrast, the process view investigates *how* internationalization takes place.

In the process view, the particular significant theory is Uppsala internationalization theory or stage theory proposed by Johanson and Wiedersheim-Paul (1975). In their model, a firm's internationalization is seen as a process in which the enterprise gradually increases its international involvement. This process evolves between the development of knowledge about foreign markets and an increasing commitment of resources to foreign markets. In their study of four Swedish firms, they observed that when firms internationalized, they followed a series of incremental steps. They identified the following four stages:

1. No regular export activities;
2. Export via independent agent;
3. Establishment of a foreign sales subsidiary;
4. Establishment of a foreign manufacturing plant

The Uppsala internationalization theory is based on assumptions pertaining to the relations among market commitment, market knowledge, current business activities, and commitment decisions. During internationalization, market entries are supported at first with physically close and geographically close markets. Over time and through experience, firms will increase their international commitment. This increased commitment, in turn, will enhance market knowledge, which leads to further commitment in more distant markets.

The internationalization process model can explain two patterns in the internationalization of a firm (Johanson & Wiedersheim-Paul, 1975). One is that the firm's engagement in the specific country, the international market develops according to an establishment chain, i. e. no regular export activities are performed in the market at the start, and then exports take place via independent representatives, later through a sales subsidiary, and eventually manufacturing may follow. These sequential stages indicate an increasing market resource commitment. The second pattern has firms enter new markets with successively greater psychic distance. Psychic distance refers to factors such as difference in language, culture, and political systems which disturb flow of information between the firm and the market (Vahlne & Wiedersheim-Paul, 1975). Thus, firms start internationalization by going to those markets they can most easily understand.

Overall, the model has gained strong support in studies of a wide spectrum of countries and situations. The empirical research confirms that commitment and experience are important factors for explaining international business behavior. The model is not limited to countries like Sweden which are rather small and highly industrialized. Later research from other counties has reported empirical observations in support of or consistent with the model. Empirical research by Wisconsin researchers about export behavior provides a similar picture (Bilkey, 1978; Bilkey & Tesar, 1978; Cavusgil, 1980; 1984). Consistent results have also been reported from extensive export research in Mannheim (Dichtl et al., 1984). Denis and Depelteau (1985) have also reported supporting results from empirical studies of market selections of US firms going abroad. Similar results have also been obtained in studies of Hawaiian export firms (Hook &

Czinkota, 1988), Japanese firms' export strategies (Johansson & Nonaka, 1983), Turkish exporters (Karafakioglu, 1986), and Australian firms (Barrett, 1986).

The stage theory is influential in the internalization and has gained considerable support from a large majority of international business literature. However, it also received some criticism. Welch and Loustarinen (1988) reports about small English firms, Australian start-ups, and established Swedish firms that skipped important stages and were involved with unexpected speed in direct foreign investments. In addition, Sullivan and Bauerschmidt (1990) found that a firm's stage of international involvement was an unexpectedly poor predictor of European managers' knowledge and beliefs. Moreover, in a study of Swedish firms in Janpan, Hedlund and Kverneland (1985) found evidence that the development patterns of those firms were not in accordance with those expected on the basis of the internationalization process model. The reason for this is that there has been a general internationalization of industries and markets so that the lack of market knowledge is not an important factor limiting the space and patterns of firm's internationalization. Forsgren (1989) claims that the Uppsala model is valid only in the early stages of the internationalization process, when a lack of market knowledge and market resources is still a constraining force.

The world has become much more homogeneous and that consequently psychic distance has decreased. Especially, a "born global" firms or international new ventures give a big challenge to the incremental theory. However, despite the short-coming of stage theory, it still made a major contribution that the international business growth is step-wise owing to the limited resource and market knowledge.

Actually, Johanson and Vahlne (1990) dismissed these concerns as merely indicative of the need for adjustment to their model of firm internationalization. First, firms with large resources are expected to take large steps toward internationalization. Second, when foreign market conditions are stable and homogeneous, learning about them is easier. Third, when firms have considerable experience with markets that are similar to newly targeted foreign markets, previous experience may be generalizable to the new arena. However, none of the exceptions seem to apply to international new ventures. Moreover, their resources are constrained by their young age and small size. Therefore, according to Johanson and Vahlne's (1990) own standards, stage theory needs more than a minor adjustment.

2.1.2 Network Theory

With increased global competition and accelerating technological development, firms are forced to internationalize more rapidly than they used to be. Old models of incremental internationalization are no longer valid (Bilkey & Teasar, 1978; Johanson & Vahlne, 1977; Cavusgil, 1980; Welch & Luostarinen, 1988). Interestingly, the network perspective has evolved from Johanson and Vahlne's early work, and reflects their ongoing research exploring the management of foreign market entry. Johanson and Vahlne (1992) found that although foreign market entry is a gradual process (supporting the Uppsala model), it results from interaction, and the development and maintenance of relationship over time. Therefore, most research began to place attention on networks when trying to understand and explain the rapid internationalization.

The network perspective is drawn on the theories of social exchange and resource dependency, and focuses on firm behavior in the context of a network of interorganizational and interpersonal relationships (Axelsson & Easton, 1992). According to the network perspective, the nature of relationships established between various parties will influence strategic decisions. Therefore, firms' internationalization is not only studied inside the firm itself but also in connection with its cooperation with other firms (Coviello & McAuley, 1999).

The most influential work on network theory and its relation to internationalization is provided by Johanson and Mattsson (1988). In their view, internationalization is a process that a firm applies its business networks with its customers, distributors, suppliers, competitors and government to develop and establish the international business. Johanson and Vahlne's (1992) also found that foreign market entry resulted from interaction between parties and developing relationship over time. Relationships became "bridges to foreign markets" and provided a firm with the opportunity and motivation to internationalize. Johanson and Matton (1988) also suggested that the success for firms entering foreign markets was more dependent on its position in a network and relationships than on market and cultural characteristics. Moreover, some research found that the rapid internationalization was the result of the firms' involvement in international networks. For example, Coviello and Munro (1995, 1997) identified the influence of both social and business ties on the internationalization of start-up new ventures. Similarly, Sharma and Blomstermo (2003) also found the early internationalization of two new ventures were with the help of their network relationships. Therefore, Johanson and Vahlne (2003) refined their stage theory to offer a "network model of internationalization". Overall the network perspective goes beyond the model of stage theory by suggesting that it is a network that influences a firm's internationalization.

A general assumption of network theory is that the beneficiaries of networks are small firms and at least dependent firms. Moreover, building up networks needs a lot of costs. The costs include the resources required by each firm to join the network and opportunism cost (Chetty & Campbell-Hunt, 2003). However, compared with the unilateral process suggested by stage models, the network perspective introduces a "more multilateral element" to internationalization (Johanson and Vahlne, 1992, p 12).

2.2 International Entrepreneurship Theory

2.2.1 International Entrepreneurship

The genesis of international entrepreneurial perspective is often attributed to the seminar article by Oviatt and McDougall

(1994). The authors argued that scholars in international business had largely ignored the phenomenon of international expansion by entrepreneurial firms, especially, those that internationalized early in their life cycle. While traditional international business research had focused predominantly on large, established firms, extant entrepreneurship literature had concentrated on the domestic activities of new businesses. To overcome this gap, Oviatt and McDougall (1994) provided a theoretical base for the study of international new ventures.

International new ventures were defined as business organizations "that, from inception, seek to derive significant competitive advantage from the use of resources and the sale of outputs in multiple countries" (Oviatt and McDougall, 1994 p.49). International entrepreneurship began with an interest in new ventures. One contribution of IE research has focused on the recognition of the limitations arising from the stage proposed by Johanson and Valhne (1977), to explain the INVs' phenomenon and to understand the fast speed of internationalization.

Subsequent to the article of Oviatt and McDougall (1994), additional studies were conducted and articles published: interest in the arena increased as a result. I next note some sources that demonstrate current topics of interest within the international entrepreneurship.

Firstly, the Journal of Business Venturing has published a periodic issue devoted to international entrepreneurship research. Secondly, Entrepreneurship Theory and Practice focused on international entrepreneurship in its summer 1996 issue. Thirdly, Entrepreneurship 2000, a 1997 book was edited by Don Sexton and Ray Smilor of the Center for Entrepreneurial leadership, Inc. Fourthly, a 1998 conference, "Globalization and Emerging Business: Strategies for the 21st Century" was held and it had 30 papers that addressed international entrepreneurship issues. The doctoral consortia on international entrepreneurship (IE), special issues of leading scholarly journals, workshops, the publication of handbooks and edited volumes and book chapters indicated the increasing interest in international entrepreneurship.

The meaning of the term "international entrepreneurship" has evolved over the last decade, during which academic interest in the topic has grown. In the 1990s, the focus of international entrepreneurship research was generally limited to the international activities of new ventures to the exclusion of established firms (McDougall, 1989). However, with more attention on international entrepreneurship research, recent studies start to recognize that it is desirable to expand the field to a broader scope to include established firms (McDougall & Oviatt, 2000; Zahra & George, 2002; Dess et al., 2003; Dimitrato & Jones, 2005). Over time, the definition and domain of international entrepreneurship has become more inclusive.

By the mid - 1990s, the international part of international entrepreneurship was becoming more refined. Wright and Ricks (1994) said it is firm-level business activity that crosses national borders and that such activity focuses on the relationship between business and the international environments in which they operate. Moreover, the definition of international entrepreneurship research provided by Zahra and George (2002) is "the process of creatively discovering and exploiting opportunities that lies outside of a firm's domestic market in the pursuit of competitive advantage" (p. 260). Thus, international entrepreneurship is a combination of innovative, proactive and risk-seeking behavior that crosses national borders and is intended to create value for organizations. International entrepreneurial behavior in large, established companies often was referred to as "corporate entrepreneurship".

Unlike experiential source of knowledge which is primarily gained from operations abroad (Johanson & Vahlne, 1990), the entrepreneurial source of knowledge is more likely to emanate from aggressive information acquisition activities such as active participation in international trade shows and extensive internet search (Wilkinson & Brouthers, 2000). In the entrepreneurial market-learning framework derived by Matsuno et al. , (2002) , the three dimensions of entrepreneurial proclivity — proactiveness, risk taking, and innovativeness collectively evoke a learning culture. Foreign market knowledge could be suitably acquired with greater speed from diverse sources of entrepreneurial activities that span across national borders. Thus, firms with international entrepreneurial orientation tend to have a dynamic capability to learn and internationalize early (Toyne, 1989). In this regard, international entrepreneurship gives rise to learning capabilities, permitting the sorts of assimilation and exploitation of opportunities and knowledge which otherwise have to be deployed through accumulated experience from foreign operations.

International entrepreneurship, as an organization-wide phenomenon, extends to all hierarchical levels and geographic boundaries of the firm. It is not solely an individual entrepreneur event. Moreover, it is a dynamic and evolving development process. It evolves around the discovery and exploitation of opportunities in the international marketplace. It is clear that the domain of international entrepreneurship is rich in opportunity.

Because the field is broad, there are many interesting research questions to be explored, and many existing theories may be beneficially employed.

2.2.2 Definition and Domain of International Entrepreneurship

The first fundamental issue in international entrepreneurship is the definition. International entrepreneurship relates to the two different research fields: entrepreneurship and international business, so the definition also should be jointly influenced by these two fields. Both fields also continue to evolve. Therefore, the definition of international entrepreneurship is under debate and also continues to evolve. Table2.1 presents an overview of the evolution of research about international entrepreneurship definition.

The term "international entrepreneurship" firstly appeared in Morrow (1988)'s work. In this article, it highlighted recent technological advances and cultural awareness that appeared to open previously untapped foreign markets to new ventures. However, this article did not mention the definition of international entrepreneurship.

McDougall (1989) had defined international entrepreneurship as the development of international new ventures or stat-ups that, from their inception, engage in international business. They view these firms operating domain as international from the initial stages of the firm's operation. The most influential publication of international entrepreneurship may the paper titled "Toward a theory of international new ventures" (Oviatt and McDougall, 1994). They followed previous efforts and defined international entrepreneurship as "born global". They regarded international entrepreneurship as a business organization "that, from inception, seek to derive significant competitive advantage from the use of resources and the sale of outputs in multiple countries". Thus, international entrepreneurship was still defined as "international new venture" or "born global".

However, some researchers suggested that the study of international entrepreneurship should include both new firms and established firms (Zahra, 1993; Giamartino, McDougall & Schulte, 1994). Especially, Wright and Ricks (1994) suggested that international entrepreneurship was an organizational level behavior. This definition did not use age as a criterion in defining international entrepreneurship. It highlighted that entrepreneurial activities could occur in new ventures as well as in established firms.

With the development of the definition, international entrepreneurship has evolved from a focus on new ventures to include established firms. McDougall and Oviatt (1996) recognized the importance of international entrepreneurship in established firms. They observe that international entrepreneurial firms have new and innovative activities with the goal of value creation and growth in business organizations across national borders. Subsequently, McDougall and Oviatt (2000) provided a broader definition of international entrepreneurship. They said "international entrepreneurship is a combination of innovative, proactive, and risk taking behavior that crosses national borders and is intended to create value in organization". It adopts the construct of innovation, proactiveness and risk taking behavior in international enterprise activities to measure international entrepreneurship. That is it accepted Miller's (1983) definition of entrepreneurship that focus on innovation, risk taking and proactiveness. The same with Wright and Ricks (1994)'s definition, firm size and age are not defining characteristic. Thus, corporate entrepreneurship is included in the study of international entrepreneurship. Further, international entrepreneurial behavior could occur at the individual, group and organizational level (McDougall and Oviatt, 2000).

International entrepreneurship researchers, therefore, have several important opportunities as they study established companies. New ventures and established firms work hard to foster innovation and encourage risk taking to find international market opportunities. Some researchers highlight the importance of opportunity recognition, discovery and exploitation as the distinguishing characteristics of entrepreneurship (Shane and Venkataraman, 2000). Zahra and George (2002) defined international entrepreneurship as the "the process of creatively discovering and exploiting opportunities that lie outside a firm's domestic markets in the pursuit of competitive advantage." In this definition, the term of "creatively" emphasizes the need for innovativeness during a firm's exploration foreign opportunities

Similarly, Oviatt and McDougall (2005) defined international entrepreneurship as "the discovering, enactment, evaluation, and exploitation of opportunities — across national borders — to create future goods and service" (Oviatt & McDougall, 2005; p540). This definition focused on opportunities recognition and included new ventures and corporate entrepreneurship. It also highlighted that the entrepreneurial activities are across national borders. However, this definition did not mention how many dimensions international entrepreneurship include.

With the development of international entrepreneurship, Mtigwe (2006) pointed out that the previous definitions of international entrepreneurship ignored the essence of entrepreneurship, namely, the exploitation of opportunities without regard to the resources under the firm's control. Therefore, Mtigwe (2006) provided a more inclusive definition: "a courageous managerial value creation process through which an individual engages in innovation, proactive, calculated risk-taking behavior designed to prosecute foreign business opportunities presented by multinational market success and imperfections for financial and non-financial rewards." This definition is a modification of the definition provided by McDgouall and Oviatt (2000), and it places more attention on the outcome of entrepreneurial activities.

Numerous scholars have made considerable effort at defining international entrepreneurship. However, a precise definition of international entrepreneurship still remains elusive. Most researchers agree that international entrepreneurship covers international activities of organizations regardless of age, size, private or public sector, or foreign market servicing mode. Thus, in this study, I will analyze international activities for both international new ventures and established firms.

2.2.3 International Entrepreneurship in this study

Entrepreneurial orientation is defined as the firm's predisposition to engage in entrepreneurial processes, practices, and decision making (Lumpkin & Dess, 1996; Matsuno et al., 2002). In the context of internationalization, international entrepreneurship in this study is adopted by extending the original conception to the process and activities across borders (Knight & Cavusgil, 2004). Researchers have defined international entrepreneurial orientation through the degree of innovativeness, risk taking and proactiveness of thc firm in international markets (McDougall & Oviatt, 2000; Zahra & Garvis, 2000; Mtigwe, 2006). Therefore, consistent with prior research, international entrepreneurship mainly includes three dimensions: innovativeness, proactiveness and risk-taking (Miller, 1983).

Schumpeter (1934) was among the first to emphasize the construct of innovation propensity. Innovation includes both the creation of new resources and new ways of combining available resources (Zahra et al., 1999). International innovation propensity refers to the proclivity of the firm to espouse new and creative ideas, products, or processes designed to service foreign markets (Lumpkin & Dess, 1996). Entrepreneurship encourages the pursuit of competitive advantage through introduction of innovations (Ireland et al. , 2001). Some researchers use innovativeness and entrepreneurship interchangeably because innovativeness is intrinsic to entrepreneurship (Timmons, 1978; Martin, 1984).

Proactiveness is defined as an organizational process which is directed to pursue entrepreneurial opportunities regardless of the amount of resources a firm controls (Stevenson & Gumpert, 1985; Stevenson & Jarillo, 1990). It refers to the firm's response to market opportunities, and implies an opportunity-seeking perspective (Lumpkin & Dess, 2001; Kreiser et al., 2002). Proactiveness indicates a firm's determination to pursue promising opportunities, rather than merely responding to competitors' moves (Miller, 1983). In international markets, a proactive firm will take the initiative in an attempt to shape the environment to gain a competitive advantage, and to anticipate competitors' moves and market needs.

Risk-taking behavior means the willingness to invest in projects within certain outcomes (Lumpkin & Dess, 1996). In international markets, risk taking refers to the extent to which the firm is prepared to undertake significant and risky resource commitments in foreign markets (Miller & Friesen, 1978). An international entrepreneurial firm is likely to be characterized by risk-taking behavior in order to exploit opportunities in the international marketplace (Lumpkin & Dess, 1996). During internationalization, risk attitude is conceptualized as the tendency of a firm to choose low-or high- risk projects (Khandwalla, 1977) and cautious or bold decisions when confronted with uncertainty (Naman & Slevin, 1993). Indeed, entrepreneurial firms would like to undertake a significant degree of personal, social, psychological and financial risks (Gasse, 1982; Baird & Thomas, 1985) when they face uncertainty during internationalization. If a firm is international risk-averse, it will follow the incremental mode of expansion. However, a firm with international risk taking attitude usually chooses to go abroad from inception. It would like to select to expand in physically distant countries (McDougall, 1989; Oviatt & McDougall, 1994, 1997). However, a firm may manifest international entrepreneurship in different degrees of intensity and frequency, since some firms are more innovative, proactive and risk taking than others (Covin & Slevin, 1991; Morris & Sexton, 1996).

2.3 Research Streams on International Entrepreneurship

2.3.1 Organizational Factors

Organizational factors have received more attention in the research stream on international entrepreneurship with three sets of variables widely studied i. e. top management team characteristics, firm resources, and firm specific variables. Table 2. 2 provides relevant findings about the relationship between organization factors and international entrepreneurship.

2.3.1.1 TMT Characteristics

Some researchers proposed that a global vision dating from a firm's inception is the most important characteristic associated with entrepreneurs (Oviatt & McDougall, 1995). As we know, top managers are key antecedents of a born-global firm, because it is the entrepreneur who decides whether the firm can pursue international opportunities or not (Chetty & Holm, 2000; Shrader et al., 2000, Madsen & Servais, 1997).

Top management team characteristics such as education, experience from living abroad and experience from other internationally orientated jobs mound the mind of the founder and influence the firms' international strategy (Madsen & Servais, 1997). Experience of top managers plays an important role in a firm's internationalization. Their international experiences are considered as one of the antecedents of planning internationalization (McDougall et al., 1994; Madsen & Servais, 1997). Internationally experienced management teams have a greater propensity to develop foreign strategic partners and to delay less in obtaining foreign sales after start-up, and that these behaviors are associated with the higher degree of internationalization (Reuber & Fischer, 1997).

2.3.1.2 Firm Profile

Some studies try to investigate the relationship between firm profile and internationalization. Several studies have independently found that age, as a proxy for experience, and size and scope, as proxies for excess resources and know-how, are related to the degree of commitment to international markets (Burton and Schlegelmilch, 1987; Cavusgil, 1984; Javagli et al., 1998; Verwaal & Donkers, 2002; Yang et al., 1992; Acedo, 2006). The size of a firm is perceived to be the largest barrier for non-internationalization (Shaw & Darroch, 2004; Mittelstaedt et al., 2006). However, Sapienza and Almeida (1996) found contradictroy conclusions. They found that firm size was correlated to the degree of internationalization. Firm size was considered as an indicator of managerial and financial resource availability (Dhanaraj & Beamish, 2003). Large firms looked for business opportunities abroad if excess resources are available. Whereas, small firms often lacked financial resources for investing abroad and they needed to overcome barriers such as the liability of foreignness (Coviello & McAauley, 1999; Zaheer, 1995). The larger a firm is, the higher the likelihood that it will choose to engage in internationalization. Firm profile (its age, size and scope of national operation) can reduce the entrepreneurs' perception of risk associated with internationalization (Acedo & Florin, 2006).

There are also some other profile variables listed in Table 2.3 that may influence firm internationalization. Younger firms often display an entrepreneurial mode of behavior, their management structures are more flexible and they would like to maintain a proactive attitude towards opportunity exploitation and entrepreneurial activities in the international market. Older firms with inertia would not like to take risk activities during internationalization. Moreover, new ventures have the learning advantage of newness (Autio et. 2000). They can acquire foreign market knowledge easily. Autio, Sapienza, and

Almeida (2000) identified that the age of a high-technology firm at international entry is negatively related to its subsequent growth in international sales. A firm's age at international entry is negatively related to its international learning effort (Sapienza et al., 2005).

2.3.2 Environmental Factors

Some researchers found that the market condition in which a firm operates may have a significant effect on international operations of a new venture (Oviatt & McDougall, 1994; Walters & Samiee, 1990; Madsen & Servais, 1997). For example, transportation of people and goods has become much more reliable and cheaper than ever before. This means that the cost barriers for an international approach have been removed. Similarly, because of the development of communication, world markets have become more accessible at lower costs. Therefore, these new market characteristics are the driving forces of internationalization.

Management researchers suggest that perceptions of industry complexity, heterogeneity, and turbulence affect managerial decision-making and strategies (Keiser & Sproul, 1982). As we know, heterogeneity, dynamism, and hostility are important dimensions of the external environment (Zahra & Bogner, 1999; Zahra et al., 1997). Zahra et al. (1997) suggests there was an association between a firmVs domestic environment and its export performance. When the executives of a new venture consider their environment turbulent, they are likely to intensify exporting activities and improve export performance.

Actually, external environmental factors include business systems, market-hierarchy relations, and cultural practices, within which international entrepreneurship activities are born and generated. Perceived environmental uncertainty can influence a firm's entrepreneurial strategic posture. Environmental factors may lead to the change of an entry mode in a country (Thoumrungroje & Tansuhaj, 2005; Jones & Coviello, 2005). Moreover, environmental turbulence and political culture also influence a firm's internationalization strategy (Kuivalainen et al., 2004; Armagan & Ferreira, 2005).

Previous empirical studies on these issues are shown in Table 3. Some studies failed to examine the specific attribute of the environment on international performance. However, they still think environment is one of the determinants of international entrepreneurship.

2.3.3 Strategic Factors

Researchers have investigated the effect of strategy on international entrepreneurship. The following is a summary of the key strategy variables used in prior research and their influence on international entrepreneurship.

McDougall (1989) found that the strategy content between domestic and international new venture differs. International firms emphasize marketing and grand entry strategy, whereas domestic new ventures focus more on production expansion strategy. With ongoing globalization, entrepreneurial- oriented firms tend to be more inclined to launch new ventures activities. Therefore, firms with international entrepreneurial orientation may be more inclined to implement marketing strategies (e. g. Dess, Lumpkin & Covin 1997; Khandwalla, 1977; Miller & Friesen 1984; Morris & Paul 1987). Knight (2000) also argued that the greater the firm's international entrepreneurial orientation, the more likely the firm is to pursue marketing leadership strategy, quality leadership strategy and product specialization strategy. Moreover, Knight and Cavusgil (2004) proposed that business strategies such as global technological competence, unique products development, quality focus and leveraging foreign distributor competences is a function of international entrepreneurial orientation. Unlike Knight (2000), Thoumrungroje and Tansuhaj (2005) proposed that international diversification is likely to be pursued by firms with entrepreneurial orientation because such strategy usually requires innovative, proactive, and risk-taking orientation of firms. Therefore, the more entrepreneurial the firm's strategic posture is, the greater the pursuit of the international diversification strategy (Kuivalainen, Sundqvist & Servais, 2007). This research has been devoted to the relationship between strategy and international entrepreneurship.

2.3.4 Summary of Research Streams

Extant research in international entrepreneurship explores the organizational factors such as TMT characteristics (Bloodgood, Sapienza & Almeida, 1996; McDougall & Oviatt, 1996; Oviatt & McDougall, 1995), and firm resources (Oviatt & McDougall, 1995) as the motivation of international entrepreneurship. They also investigate the influence of strategic factors such as generic strategy (McDougall, 1989; Oviatt & McDougall, 1995) and functional strategy (Bloodgood, Sapienza & Almeida, 1996; McDougall, 1989) on international entrepreneurship. However, these studies focus only on the technical and organizational level without mentioning institutional level (Parsons, 1960; Petit, 1960). Organizations are in an open system instead of a closed-system (Petit, 1960). They have to survive in their institutional environment and attempt to secure its legitimacy (Tompson, 1967). I will investigate how international entrepreneurship is influenced by a firm's institutional environment.

2.4 Chapter Summary

This chapter presents the theoretical perspectives, models, key concepts, empirical findings in the literature relating to current study. In the section 2.1, other internationalization theory such as incremental theory, network theories are reviewed. Because of the limitation of these theories, the international entrepreneurship theory is provided.

In section 2.2, research in international entrepreneurship theory was reviewed, especially about the definition of international entrepreneurship. Large research focuses on the incongruence in the definition and scope of international entrepreneurship. This section, therefore, defines the concepts and domain of international entrepreneurship. The definition provided by Oviatt and McDougall (1994) defined international entrepreneurship only in the scope of "born global" new ventures. This definition is narrow in scope. Following that, some researchers observed a need to go beyond the "born international" criterion and call for a broader definition of international entrepreneurship. More and more research defined international entrepreneurship shift attention away from using the age of the firm or timing of internationalization as the sole criterion to define international entrepreneurship. With the development of definition, established firms were also included in international entrepreneurship. Moreover, innovativeness, proactiveness and risk-taking are adopted as the three dimensions of international entrepreneurship.

In section 2. 3, research streams in international entrepreneurship were discussed. Three streams in the determining of international entrepreneurship: the organizational factor, strategic factors and environment factors. The organizational factors include some variables such as top management team characteristic, firm resources, and firm-specific variables. Strategic management and entrepreneurship researchers have long acknowledged the importance of the external environment on a firm's strategic choices. Therefore, researchers have explored the effect of a firm's external environment on different aspects of international entrepreneurship. The strategy such as generic strategy, functional strategy, entry strategy also has influence on international entrepreneurship.

The next section will present a conceptual framework and hypotheses for investing (1) What is the antecedent of international entrepreneurship (2) How international entrepreneurial firms get performance in foreign markets.

Table 2.1 A chronicle of international entrepreneurship definitions

Articles	The Definition
McDougall (1989)	International entrepreneurship is defined as the development of international new ventures or start-ups that, from their inception, engage in international business, thus viewing their operating domain as international from the initial stages of the firm's operation.
Wright & Ricks (1994)	International Entrepreneurship is a firm level activity that crosses national borders and focuses on the relationship between businesses and the international environments in which they operate.
Oviatt & McDougall (1994)	A business organization that, from inception, seeks to derive significant competitive advantage from the use of resources and sale of outputs in multiple countries.

Continued

Articles	The Definition
McDougall & Oviatt (1996)	New and innovative activities that have the goal of value creation and growth in business organization across national borders.
McDougall & Oviatt (2000)	A combination of innovative, proactive, and risk-taking behavior that crosses or is compared across national borders and is intended to create value in business organizations.
Mtigwe(2006)	A courageous managerial value creation process through which an individual engages in innovative, proactive, calculated risk-taking behavior designed to prosecute foreign business opportunities presented by multinational market successes and imperfections for financial and non-financial rewards.
Zahra & George (2002)	The process of creatively discovering and exploiting opportunities those lie outside a firm's domestic markets in the pursuit of competitive advantage.

Table 2. 2 Influence of Organizational factors on international entrepreneurship

Variables	Findings
Top management team	• Firms led by managers with foreign work experience were able to quickly internationalize their operations and do so successfully (Oviatt & McDougall, 1995; McDougall et al., 1996). • There is a positively relationship between managers' foreign work experience and degree of new venture's internationalization (Bloodgood et al., 1996; Burgel & Murray, 1998).

Continued

Variables	Findings
	• A positive relationship exists between managers receiving education outside the USA and new ventures' international expansion (Bloodgood et al., 1996). • Decision makers' cosmopolitanism has a significant influence on the initiation of exports (Ellis & Pecotich, 2001) • It shows that internationally experienced management teams have a greater propensity to develop foreign strategic partners and to delay less in obtaining foreign sales after start-up, and that these behaviors are associated with the higher degree of internationalization. (Reuber & Fischer (1997) • Firms with principal founders drawn from managerial parental backgrounds were scientifically more likely to export than firms with other types of founders (Westhead et al., 1998). • The new ventures led by managers with global visions were able to internationalize quickly and successfully (Oviatt & McDougall, 1995).
Network	• The findings suggest that the firm's network relationships are determinant with regard to which foreign entry forms they choose and to some extent, which markets they decide to enter. (Moen et al., 2004) • The paper argues that home-based social networks play a mediating role in the relationship between inward and outward internationalization and firm performance. (Zhou et al., 2007) • Internal and external social capital influences the acquisition and creation of knowledge, and that knowledge is a key resource driving the international growth of TBNFs. (Yli-Renko et al., 2002)

Continued

Variables	Findings
	• In financing decisions relating to INVs, venture capitalists and other venture financiers should look for entrepreneurs who have a global vision, international business competence. (McDougall et al., 1994) • The perceived usefulness of network experiential knowledge, its antecedents, and its performance effects in the internationalization process of firms. (Blomstermo et al., 2004) • Networking capability enables identification and exploitation of foreign market opportunities, facilities international market performance in the born global firm. (Mort et al., 2006) • Knowledge of foreign market opportunities is commonly acquired via existing interpersonal links rather than collected systematically via market research (Ellis, 2000) • The importance networks in the internationalization of entrepreneurial firms are widely accepted. Loane, & Bell, 2006) • During internationalization, networks can help firms expose themselves to new opportunities, obtain knowledge, learn from experiences, and benefit from the synergistic effect of pooled resources. (Chetty & Holm, 2000) • The network moderates the speed of internationalization. (Oviatt & McDougall, 2005) • The study examines the influence of network relationship on the internationalization process of small firms. These relationships impact foreign market selection and model of entry, as well as product development and market diversification activities. (Coviello & Munro, 1997) • new ventures with extensive network were able to internationalize quickly and successfully (Oviatt and McDougall, 1995) • Technological networks are positively and significantly associated with status, speed, and degree of internationalization. (Zahra et al, 2006).

Continued

Variables	Findings
	• Network relationships of high technology firm can help pursue foreign market opportunities and conduct international market activities (Coviello et al., 1995) • Firms that had received industry grants were significantly more likely to export (Westhead et al., 1998). • The authors argue that network should be considered in the international entrepreneurship study (Welch et al., 2004)
Size	• Firm size is positively associated with degree of internationalization (Bloodgood et al., 1996; Zahra et al., 2000) • High-tech startups that internationalized were significantly larger in sales and employment than firms that did not internationalize (Burgel & Murray, 1998). • There was no significant difference in employment of exporters vs. non-exporters (Westhead et al., 1998).
Location	• There was no significant difference between firms that exported and those that did not in rural vs. urban location (Westhead et al., 1998) • National culture influences the formation of technology alliances by entrepreneurial firms (Steensma et al., 2000).
Organizational Learning	• Experiential learning and systematic planning moderate the Small and Medium-sized Enterprises' internationalization (Li, 2004).

Table 2.3 Influences of Strategic Factors on International Entrepreneurship

Variables	Findings
Generic Strategy • Low cost • Differentation	• Product differentiation was important for rapid internationalization (Oviatt & McDougall, 1995). • Product differentiation is positively associated with degree of internationalization (Bloodgood et al., 1996). • Unique product is important for internationalization (Fontes & Coombs, 1997). • R&D spending positively and significantly associated with international collaborative relationships which were positively and significantly associated with absolute annual international sales growth (Autio et al., 1997).
Functional Strategy Production Distribution Marketing	• International new ventures emphasize a distribution and marketing strategy less than domestic ventures (McDougall, 1989). • Firms that had the majority of their customers located in the same country as those measured six years earlier were significantly less likely to export (Westhead et al., 1998). • A negative sign (marginally significant) between marketing differentiation and degree of internationalization (Bloodgood et al., 1996).
Entry Strategy	• International new ventures emphasized grand entry sale significantly more than domestic ventures (McDougall, 1989). • Firms that targeted niche markets composed of clients were prepared to internationalize (Fontes & Coombs, 1997). • Technology alliances by entrepreneurial firms affected by national culture (Steensma et al., 2000).

Continued

Variables	Findings
	• The findings reveal that born-global firms leverage a distinctive mix of orientations, and strategies that allow them to succeed in diverse international markets. (Knight el., 2004) • Technology-based international new ventures had significantly different strategies than similar ventures that sold their products only domestically (McDougall & Oviatt, 1996). • The strategy of international new ventures are significantly different from domestic new ventures (McDougall, 1989)

Table 2. 4 Influences of Environment Factors on International Entrepreneurship

Variables	Findings
Intensity of domestic competition	• Domestic market saturation was mentioned by only 26 of responding firms as a motivation for internationalization (Karagozoglu & Lindell, 1998). • No difference between international and purely domestic new venture (McDougall, 1989).
Limited domestic Growth	• Limited growth of domestic markets was a major reason for the rapid internationalization of high-technology new venture (Coviello & Munro, 1995). • Insufficiency of domestic sales to achieve competitive level of R&D was key motivation to internationalization. (Karagozoglu & Lindell, 1998).

Continued

Variables	Findings
Intensity of international competition	• International new ventures competed in industries that exhibited significantly higher levels of international competition (McDougall, 1989).
Institutional environment	• Institutional environment significantly influence international entrepreneurship (Mitchell et al., 2000) • Institutional structures in emerging economies facilitate entrepreneurship through effective governance mechanisms (George & Prabhu, 2000)
Economies of scale	• No differences between international and domestic new venture (McDougall, 1989).
Retaliation by industry incumbents	• No differences between international domestic new ventures (McDougall, 1989).
Industry gross profits	• Is negatively and significantly associated with degree of internationalization (Bloodgood et al., 1996)
Industry sales growth	• Positively (not significant) associated with degree of internationalization (Bloodgood et al., 1996)
Type of industry	• Service firms tended to internationalize less than manufacturing firms (Burgel & Murray, 1998; Westhead et al., 1998).
Environment turbulence	• Environmental turbulence is a better indicator of international performance in knowledge-intensive firms than in others. (Kuivalainen et al., 2004)
Environmental hostility	The relationship between ICE and firm performance is moderated by environmental hostility. (Oviatt & McDougall, 2005)

Continued

Variables	Findings
Export market orientation	• Exporter's market orientation enhances the cooperation between the exporters and their major overseas distributor while minimizing their dependence and relationship distance. (Racela, et al., 2007)
Environmental uncertainty	Environmental uncertainty is hypothesized to strengthen the relationship between a firm's a firm's entrepreneurial strategic posture and international diversification strategy, which ultimately affect the firm's performance. (Thoumrungroje, et al., 2005).

Chapter 3
Theoretical Framework and Hypotheses

The purpose of this study is to gain a deeper understanding on antecedents of international entrepreneurship as well as the role of international entrepreneurship in the internationalization of firms. Drawing on neoinstitutional theory, this study first proposes that the internationalization of the organizational field is an important antecedent of international entrepreneurship. In China, the increasing internationalization of organizational fields provides firms with legitimacy to be of international entrepreneurship. Subsequently, based on the role of knowledge in internationalization and the exploitation-exploration learning, this chapter proposes that international entrepreneurship mediate the relationship between organizational field and exploitative and exploratory learning. Thirdly, according to exploitation-exploration learning model, the inverted-U shape relationship between exploitative learning and performance and exploratory learning and performance are presented.

3.1 Theoretical Framework

3.1.1 Institutional theory in international entrepreneurship

3.1.1.1 Ncoinstitutional theory

DiMaggio and Powell (1983) propose that organizations increasingly become prisoners in the new "iron cage" of institutional isomorphism. The trend toward conformity is a central element of the neoinstitutional perspective. To describe the process of homogenization, DiMaggio and Powell (1983) adopted the ecological concept of isomorphism. A fundamental consequence of institutional isomorphism is the acceptance of an organization by its external environment (DiMaggio & Powell, 1983; Meyer & Rowan, 1977; Meyer & Scott, 1983). Organizational characteristics such as structures, practices and strategies (Meyer & Rowan, 1977; Tolbert & Zucker, 1983) are all subject to isomorphism.

DiMaggio and Powell (1983) developed the notion that organizations exist in the fields of other organizations that may influence their behavior. In neoinstitutional terms, the environment is conceptualized as an organizational field. The field determines the patterns of organizational structures and actions. Organizational filed is defined as those organizations that, on aggregate, constitute a recognized area of institutional life: key suppliers, resources and product consumers, regulatory agencies, and other organizations that produce similar services or products (DiMaggio and Powell, 1983). It encompasses both populations of competing organization and interorganizational relationships (Powell and DiMaggio, 1991). When a field well is established, there will be an inexorable push towards homogenization. That is when an organization is structured into an actual field, powerful forces will lead the firm to become more similar to other organization in the organizational field (DiMaggio and Powell 1983; Meyer and Rowan 1997; Scott, 1987).

DiMaggio and Powell (1983) argue that this continuing push toward isomorphism may be due to a number of institutional processes: coercive isomorphism, mimetic isomorphism and normative isomorphism. The coercive isomorphism results from both formal and informal pressures exerted on an organization by other organizations upon which they are dependent and by cultural expectation in their society. The mimetic isomorphism comes from standard response to uncertainty (DiMaggio and Powell, 1983). It is a process that organizations change over time to become more similar to other organizations in their environment. When organizational technologies are poorly understood, when goals are ambiguous, or when the environment creates symbolic uncertainty, organization would like to model themselves on other organizations. The normative isomorphism stems primarily from professionalization that involves two processes. First, members of professions receive similar training, which socializes them into similar worldview. Second, members of professions interact through professional and trade associations, which further diffuse ideas among them (Larson, 1977; Collins, 1979; DiMaggio &Powell, 1983).

3.1.1.2 Neoinstitutional theory in international entrepreneurship study

The traditional economic theory of the firm treats the firm as a closed and deterministic system. However, some economists take the firm as open systems. They think the firm is a reactive entity rather than the active in the traditional theory. In the open system, the firm consciously and unconsciously adapts to changing environmental conditions to survive (Cyert & March, 1963). In this study, I follow the composite system viewpoint. In this view, the firm retains the rationality assumption of uncertainty and drive for survival of the open-system view. Therefore, the firm is not unable to operate with complete rationality nor must it face complete uncertainty.

According to Parsons' theory of organization there are three levels of responsibility and control in the firm — technical, organization, and institutional. The technical level is a subsystem which produces the goods or services which are the firm's output. The organizational level controls and services the technical level. The institutional level deals with the relation of the firm to its environment. It maintains good relations with the public, the industry, government — any group, or organization, or institution whose support is required for the firm's survival.

Extant research in international entrepreneurship explores the organizational factors such as TMT characteristics (Bloodgood, Sapienza & Almeida, 1996; McDougall & Oviatt, 1996; Oviatt & McDougall, 1995), and firm resources (Oviatt & McDougall, 1995) as the motivation of international entrepreneurship. Some studies also investigate the influence of strategic factors such as generic strategy (McDougall, 1989; Oviatt & Mc-

Dougall, 1995) and functional strategy (Bloodgood, Sapienza, Almeida, 1996; McDougall, 1989) on international entrepreneurship. Relative research has been mentioned in Chapter 2. However, these studies focus only on the technical and organizational level without mentioning institutional level (Parsons, 1960; Petit, 1960). According to the Parsons' theory of the organizational three levels, not only the technical and organization level should be considered in international entrepreneurship, the institutional level needs more attention in a firm's internationalization. Thercforc, in this study, thc ncoinstitutional theory is applied to analyze international entrepreneurship.

3.1.2 Organizational learning in international entrepreneurship

3.1.2.1 The role of organizational learning in international entrepreneurship

A critical consideration in internationalization is the knowledge problem between a firm's existing resources and those needing in a particular foreign market (Johanson and Vahlne, 1977; Madhok 1996, 1997). In the 1970s, Johanson and Colleagues (Johanson & Vahlne, 1977; Johanson & Wiedersheim-Paul, 1975) argue that a firm's market knowledge determines its internationalization. The internationalization theory puts knowledge at the center of the internationalization process. According to Eriksso, Johanson, Majkgard & Sharma (1997), lack of foreign market knowledge is a significant obstacle to a firm's internationalization. The knowledge is a necessary driver in a firm's successfully internationalization (Bikey & Tesar, 1978; Simmonds & Smith, 1968). Moreover, it is also vital in dealing with environmental uncertainties in firm internationalization (Liesch & Knight, 1999) and informing decisions on market selection, mode of choice and pace of internationalization (Young et al., 1989). A lack of foreign knowledge is a significant obstacle to firms' internationalization (Eriksson et al., 1997). Therefore, the Uppsala Model proposed that the vital role of organization learning in firms' internationalization. However, these authors emphasize experiential learning. Knowledge whatever experiential or objective knowledge is the determination of internationalization. The difference is that objective knowledge can be taught; the experience knowledge can only be learned through personal experience.

This study is based on the knowledge view of internationalization. Moreover, I agree that the accumulation of knowledge through learning constitutes a driving force in firms' internationalization (Penrose, 1959; Spender & Grant, 1996). Actually, organizational learning is an important issue for all types of firms, especially for international firms. The learning activities are granted as a process of knowledge acquisition, knowledge assimilation, and knowledge exploitation (Argote, 1999; Cohen & Levinthal, 1990; Huber, 1991). A learning organization is one "skilled in creating, acquiring, and transferring knowledge and modifying its behavior to reflect new knowledge and insights" (Garvin, 1993 p80). In order to get foreign knowledge, a firm has to take great effort at learning activities.

3.1.2.2 Exploitative and Exploratory Learning

Organizational learning effort pertains to activities aimed at both building on existing knowledge and developing new knowledge (Cohen & Levinthal, 1990). Therefore, it pertains to two different activities: exploitation learning and exploration learning (Cohen & Levinthal 1990; Levinthal & March, 1993). Exploitative learning aims at building on existing knowledge. Exploratory learning devotes on developing new knowledge. Exploitation involves the incremental improvement of existing knowledge, skills and processes, whereas exploratory learning involves the activities of searching new knowledge. Exploration includes things captured by terms such as search, variation, experimentation, discovery etc. (March, 1991). However, exploitation includes such things as refinement, choice, production, efficiency, selection etc.

Firms that focus only on exploration and exclude the exploitation would likely suffer the costs of experimentation without gaining the benefits. In contrast, firms that engage in exploitation to the exclusion exploration are likely to find themselves trapped in suboptimal stable equilibrium (March, 1991). Exploitation learning may not be sufficient in the long run to maintain a competitive advantage, since the environment in which an organization operates changes over time. Therefore, a firm has to take organizational learning effort as both exploit existing knowledge and to explore for new knowledge. Maintaining an appropriate balance between exploration and exploitation is a primary factor in firms' survival and prosperity in their internationalization Levinthal and March (1993).

3.2 Development of the hypotheses

3.2.1 The antecedent of international entrepreneurship

Organizations face the pressure of "institutional isomorphism" to conform to forms, strategies and process deemed legitimate by its external environment (DiMaggio & Powell, 1983). As mentioned before, in institutional terms, the environment is conceptualized as an organizational field. Organizational field is "those organization that, in the aggregate, constitute a recognized area of institutional life' (DiMaggio & Powell, 1983: p. 148). Once a field becomes well established, there is an inexorable isomorphic push (DiMaggio & Powell, 1983; DiMaggio, 1983). Organizations in the field face this pressure to conform to certain norms, since violating them may call into the legitimacy question and thus affect their ability to secure resources and social support (DiMaggio & Powell, 1983; Powell & DiMaggio, 1991; Tolbert, 1985). Thc cxistcncc of isomorphic pull may come through coercive, mimetic, and normative pressures from their organizational fields which induce firms to take on international entrepreneurial activities (DiMaggio & Powell, 1983).

Coercive isomorphism is driven by the pressures from other organizations in their fields and the organization's pressure to conform to the cultural expectations of the larger society (DiMaggio & Powell, 1983; Mizruchi & Fein, 1999). In China, the government has already begun to establish certain policies to encourage internationalization. For example, in 1992, Deng Xiaoping's journey to the South had brought Chinese internationalization to a new stage. In 1998, "go out" strategy is formalized in the 10th five-year plan. After joining the WTO, the social expectation for internationalization is stronger and China is more eager to integrate into the global environment. In 11th five-year plan Chinese government emphasized again the necessity of "go out" for Chinese firms. Currently, more and more Chinese firms devote to go out and pursue international opportunities. According to neoinstitutional theory, organizations will be awarded for being similar to other organizations in their fields. The similarity can make it easier for firms to transact with other organizations, to attract career-minded staff etc. (DiMaggio & Powell, 1983; Powell & DiMaggio 1991). Thus, with the internationalization of organizational field and the strong social expectation of going abroad, the coercive isomorphism motivates firms to model themselves after other organizations and go abroad.

Mimetic isomorphism is a response to uncertainty (DiMaggio & Powell, 1983). There are some uncertainties during internationalization because organizations are unfamiliar with and lack roots in a host country. In order to overcome this liability, firms would like to imitate other successful organizational practices.

Normative isomorphism is a result of professionalization (DiMaggio & Powell, 1983). Some researchers have found that the education and working experience of entrepreneurs influence international entrepreneurship (Bloodgood et al., 1996; Oviatt, & McDougal, 1995; Westhead & Ucbasaran, 1998). However, these studies are only from the firm resource perspective. From the institutional isomorphism perspective, when entrepreneurs receive similar training, which socializes them into similar worldviews. Moreover, entrepreneurs also interact through professional and trade association and diffuse their ideas. Therefore, the normative isomorphism pushes a firm to take entrepreneurial activities.

It is noteworthy that innovation can be accounted for in isomorphism (DiMaggio & Powell, 1983). Firms can adopt innovation to enhance legitimacy. Moreover, isomorphism does not exclude proactiveness, which is a firm's determination to pursue promising opportunities, rather than merely responding to competitors' moves (Miller, 1983). However, isomorphism does not only come from competitors but also from other actors in their organizational field because organizations also imitate other actors besides their domestic competitors. The opposite of proactiveness is passiveness that is of indifference or an inability to seize opportunities or lead in the market place (Lumpkin & Dess, 1996). However, it is not passive behavior when firms take international entrepreneurial behavior to achieve legitimacy.

Currently, with the growth of foreign competitors in China, domestic competitors, suppliers, and customers going abroad, some organizational fields in China are becoming more international. With the organizational field expanding geographically, isomorphism pressure of internationalization has commenced. Thus, the increasingly internationalization of their organizational fields provides firms with legitimacy to be international entrepreneurship. The greater the pressure for internationalization from their organizational fields, the more likely the firm will take international entrepreneurial activities. Therefore, operating in an international organization field tends to be a predictor of international entrepreneurship. Thus, I hypothesize that:

H1: The internationalization of organizational field is the antecedent of international entrepreneurship.

3.2.2 The mediating effects: international entrepreneurship in exploitative and exploratory learning

After firms go abroad, a new question arises as to how international entrepreneurial firms survive in a foreign environment. In effect, the international firms confront two distinct sets of isomorphic pressure, i. e. domestic market and host country. These two distinct sources of legitimacy determine the behavior of organizations. Before firms go abroad, the isomorphic pressure in the domestic market pushes firms to demonstrate international entrepreneurship. After firms go abroad, the legitimacy pressure from host country dominates firms' behaviors. Besides the objective reason for achieving legitimacy, the subjective reason is that international entrepreneurial firms also provide the learning culture for acquiring host country knowledge. External pressure and the firm's competence make us contend that international entrepreneurship is positively related to these two kinds of learning. I provide the following rationale for my claim.

One reason of the liability of foreignness arises from the lack of legitimacy in host country (Zaheer, 1995). Host country specific knowledge is a driving force behind international expansion performance (Barkema & Vermeulen, 1997; Inkpen & Beamish, 1997). They may include knowledge about business norms and law, potential customers and competitors and issues of operation management in host country (Craig & Douglas, 1996). In order to get legitimacy and compete with local firms, firms have to devote to learning activities for acquiring host country specific knowledge which influences a firm's ability to adapt its product to the local market condition.

Organizational learning localized in an overseas setting is a process of knowledge acquisition and assimilation. In other words, a firm can achieve legitimacy by devoting itself to organization learning to acquire host country specific knowledge. As a result, international firms' intrinsic disadvantages due to lack of legitimacy can be substantially overcome.

As mentioned before, a firm's learning of foreign knowledge can be distinguished by its motivation to either exploit its existing knowledge or to look for new knowledge about the host country (March, 1991). Consistent with March's model, I classify organizational learning into exploitative learning and exploratory learning. Exploitative learning is based upon the firm's existing resource to acquire host country knowledge and exploratory learning is the propensity to acquire knowledge not related to current resources (March, 1991). Considering that maintaining adaptiveness requires both exploiting existing competencies and exploring new ones (Floyd & Lane, 2000), international entrepreneurial firms will carry out these two kinds of learning activities to acquire host country knowledge.

Acquiring knowledge for obtaining legitimacy is the objective pressure from host country. From the subjective perspective, international entrepreneurial firms also provide the learning culture for acquiring host country knowledge.

International entrepreneurship is a firm's disposition to engage in innovative, proactive and risk-taking activities in its internationalization (Knight & Cavusgil, 2004; Zhou, 2007). It provides the culture for exploitative learning (Matsuno, Mentzer & Ozsomer, 2002). That is to say, an international entrepreneurial firm will establish relative rules and norms for expanding efforts toward supporting innovative, proactive and risk-taking activities for exploiting existing resources to acquire host country knowledge. In other words, an international entrepreneurial firm seeks to apply prior knowledge and existing resources such as social capital to exploit host country knowledge (Johanson & Mattson, 1988). The three dimensions of international entrepreneurship collectively facilitate the firm's willingness and ability to engage in exploitative learning. Therefore, I propose that:

H2: International entrepreneurship is positively related to exploitative learning.

H3: International entrepreneurship mediates the relationship between the internationalization of organizational field and exploitative learning.

Innovativeness includes fostering a spirit of creativity and experimentation (Lumpkin & Dess, 2001). Specifically, an innovative firm tends to be non-conventional and creative and it can identify innovative business opportunities. Entrepreneurial activities influence exploratory learning by increasing a firm's commitment to innovative ideas and products. Proactiveness refers to a forward-looking perspective to take initiative by anticipating and pursuing new opportunities (Lumpkin & Dess, 1996), which indicates a firm's determination to pursue promising international opportunities and seek host country knowledge. Therefore, the greater the proactiveness is, the greater a firm's exploratory learning efforts. In terms of risk-taking, it is the willingness of a firm to pursue host country specific knowledge that might lead to costly failure. Entrepreneurial firms will understand the risks and attempt to manage the risks to acquire knowledge (Miller & Friesen, 1980). In fact, without risk taking, knowledge acquisition in the host country may be extremely limited (Eriksson, et al. 1997). In particular, "timid" firms may not make the learning effort. Therefore, the following hypotheses are proposed:

H4: International entrepreneurship is positively related to exploratory learning.

H5: International entrepreneurship mediates the relationship between the internationalization of organizational field and exploratory leaning.

3.2.3 The effects of exploitative and exploratory learning in performance

Levinthal and March (1993) argue that the survival of a firm is dependent upon the firm's ability to "engage in enough exploitation" and "engage in enough exploration". Exploitative learning involves the use of resources the firm already has (Lyles & Schwenk, 1992; March, 1991). During internationalization, firms engage in some activities to use their existing resources to get host country knowledge.

Exploitative learning arises out of a necessity for firms to fully use their limited resources. This can reduce errors and avoid mistakes in internationalization and allow firms to select and modify the best mix of technology and production methods that meet the particular institutional environment and customers abroad (Eriksson et al. 2000). Therefore, exploitative learning enables firms to improve performance by building on and replicating prior or existing knowledge and experience. However, a high level of exploitation implies that a firm may lack the volume and diversity of new knowledge about host country that deviates substantially from current knowledge (Atuahene-Gima & Murray, 2007). Deep exploitative learning may not be harmful in the short run. But in the long run, it may reduce the firm's ability to discover opportunities and respond to environmental changes and make the adoption of new directions of development difficult. Thus, excessive exploitation may lead to inefficiency and errors in a host country because of "familiarity traps" (Ahuja & Lampert, 2001) and "organizational myopia" (Audia et al., 2000; March, 1991).

In summary, although exploitation may make firm get legitimacy and enhance performance in foreign markets, beyond a certain point, it results in lower performance because of knowledge ossification. Thus, I propose that:

H6: Exploitative learning has an inverted U-shaped relationship with firm performance in foreign markets, such that the positive effect decreases after a threshold level.

During the process of internationalization, a firm also explores new knowledge beyond its existing capabilities and resources, which is exploratory learning. Exploratory learning is a highly uncertain and unpredictable activity, reflecting the ability of a firm to acquire new knowledge rather than merely learning how to use current knowledge more efficiently (March, 1991).

Exploration enhances performance because it increases firms' new variants of knowledge in the knowledge repertoire (March, 1991). By providing new knowledge about host country, exploration ensures that firms adapt to foreign environment and get legitimacy. Despite these advantages, there are high risks and costs associated with exploration. In addition, firms also should take time to understand and assimilate the knowledge. However, because of their absorptive capacity, firms do not fully understand new knowledge. Even though they assimilate knowledge, limited resources may make firms fail in internationalization. I contend that risks and cost of exploration may reduce firms' performance in foreign markets. Therefore, excessive exploration results in high costs from failed experiments and insufficient rewards from successful ones.

In brief, although exploration may be beneficial, after a

certain point, it can diminish performance. Thus, exploratory learning has an inverted U-shaped relationship to performance, such that at low levels, its effect on performance is positive, but at a higher level, its effect on international performance tends to be negative.

H7: Exploratory learning has an inverted U-shaped relationship with performance, such that the positive effect decreases after a threshold level.

3.3 Chapter Summary

In this chapter I first discuss the neoinstitutional theory, which provides a theoretical basis for expecting the relationship between the organizational field and international entrepreneurship. Then, I discuss the role of knowledge in firm internationalization. Furthermore, I provide the two learning activities: explorative learning and exploratory learning. These activities can be employed for firms to acquire knowledge for firm internationalization. Finally, hypotheses are proposed. Based upon neoinstitutinal theory, I propose that the internationalization of organizational field is the antecedent of international entrepreneurship. With the organizational field expanding geographically, isomorphism pressure of internationalization has commenced. Thus, in China, the increasingly internationalization of their organizational fields provide firms with legitimacy to be international entrepreneurship. The greater the pressure for internationalization from their organizational fields, the more likely the firm will take international entrepreneurial activities. Therefore, operating in an international organization field tends to be a predictor of international entrepreneurship. An international entrepreneurial firm will establish relative rules and norms for expanding efforts toward supporting innovative, proactive and risk-taking activities for exploiting existing resources to acquire host country knowledge. I also provided that international entrepreneurship mediates the effects of international entrepreneurship and two kinds of learning activities. Furthermore, I also provide the inverted-U shape learning activities and performance.

The model presented in Figure 1. 1 encompasses the entire relationship hypothesized between the internationalization of organizational field, international entrepreneurship, exploitative learning, exploratory learning and performance. Table 3. 1 provides a summary of all the proposed hypotheses underlying the relationships presented in Figure 1. 1.

Table 3.1 Summary of Study Hypotheses

	Hypotheses
H1	The internationalization of organizational field is the antecedent of international entrepreneurship.
H2	International entrepreneurship is positively related to exploitative learning.
H3	International entrepreneurship mediates the relationship between the organizational field and exploitative learning.
H4	International entrepreneurship is positively related to exploratory learning.
H5	International entrepreneurship mediates the relationship between organizational field and exploratory leaning.
H6	Exploitative learning has an inverted U-shaped relationship with firm performance in foreign markets, such that the positive effect decreases after a threshold level.
H7	Exploratory learning has an inverted U-shaped relationship with performance, such that the positive effect decreases after a threshold level.

Chapter 4
Research Methodology

This research involves the examination of the relationship among the internationalization of organization field, international entrepreneurship, exploitative and exploratory learning, and performance. Chapter 4 presents the theoretical framework and research hypotheses. This chapter aims to describe the methodology used to provide data to investigate them. It covers (1) sample (2) data collection (3) questionnaire and measures (4) reliability and validity assessment and (5) analysis methods.

4.1 Sample

The study aims to examine international entrepreneurship in

the context of the Chinese economy.

First, as mentioned in Chapter 1, only firms which are involved in exporting or some other international activities are considered in this study.

Second, according to the definition of international entrepreneurship, international new venture and established firms are both included in this study. Therefore, the age of the international firms is not a problem.

Thirdly, in order to ensure a stable operating structure and availability of data on firm performance, the firms that employ at least forty people and have been operating at least three years are considered in this study.

Fourth, the sample firms operate in a wide variety of industries. This is beneficial because the purpose of this study tries to generalize beyond a few particular industries, to the population of for-profit organizations.

Fifth, considering China's large area and the economic gap between different regions, I collected data in five municipalities, namely Shanghai, Beijing, Shandong, Wuhan and Shenzhen. The five locations were carefully selected based on their level of economic development.

Finally, the respondents were from the top management

teams, not limited to the CEO. They held responsibilities for exporting or similar types of international activities in their firms.

The sample frame was provided by the association of export firms in each city. In this frame, considering the cost of time and money, the study adopted the availability sampling method (Keppel, Saufley & Tokunaga, 1992) rather than random sampling. This is also a limitation of this study, because the main problem of the availability sampling method is that it is difficult to know how representative the sample population is.

4.2 Data Collection

4.2.1 Pilot study

The questionnaire was developed on the basis of an extensive literature review. Previous studies on institutional environment, organizational learning and international entrepreneurship are the basis for developing the questionnaire. The details about how to measure the variables will be provided in the "Measures" section.

Most of the measurement scales are from Western studies. In order to ensure the measurement scales retained their psychometric properties when employed in China, structured interviews were conducted with 3 entrepreneurs from international firms. The interview questions focused on the issues concerning institutional environment, learning activities in internationalization, international entrepreneurship and performance. After that, I summarized each interview and coded each subject's answers to the issue identified from the literature. From this, I modified the questionnaire so that each question could be adapted to Chinese context. The questionnaire was originally in English and then translated into Chinese.

After developing the questionnaire, a pretest study was carried out in July 2008 in Shanghai. In order to improve the content validity of the measurement, the marketing managers of 12 Chinese firms were required to check item wording and verify the ability of the items to tap the major constructs. If a manager objected to an item, the item was either reworded or deleted from the final questionnaire.

Appendix 1 and 2 are the final questionnaire in English and Chinese. The questionnaire includes five parts. They are separately Part A: International entrepreneurship; Part B: International learning effect; Part C: Internationalization of organizational field; Part D: Performance; Part E: Company

Background.

4.2.2 Final Data Collection

In China, survey data collection has frequently been hampered by a high non-response rate and a reluctance to be interviewed. Some international researchers already mentioned this serious problem (Calantone, Schmidt & Song, 1996). Thus, in order to improve the response rate, I took the following measures to carry out this survey.

First, a research team was organized to monitor the data collection. Given the time and financial constrains, ten postgraduate students from a reputable university in Wuhan were employed to help me during the data collection. These students were recommended by an associate professor who was responsible for marketing surveys. These students were trained on all aspects of the questionnaire and how to conduct this survey.

Second, to improve participation, the methods of field interview and main survey were both applied in the data collection. Firstly, the research assistant contacted the managers by telephone. In the call, they emphasized that all the data would be used for academic research and that we guaranteed the confidentiality. Some of the managers agreed to participate in personal interviews; some asked for the questionnaire to be mailed to them. However, there were also some people who did not want to be involved in this survey. Research assistants interviewed the people who did agree to take part. Where possible, the interviewees were required to complete the questionnaire during the interview. For others, research assistants mailed the questionnaire to them and made a follow-up call one week later to remind them to fill out the questionnaire.

Third, the study chooses members from the top management teams rather than just CEOs. The general manager was viewed as the most qualified informant who could provide a valid response to questions about the organization-level construct. However, considering the response rate and data collection difficulties, I chose people who were in top management teams as the respondents. Top management team here refers to those members who had actively participated in export decision making. Top management team such as the marketing manager and business manager often played an important role in international marketing. It is thus believed that members from top management teams are knowledgeable about international marketing strategy and performance. Therefore, in the questionnaire, it was noted that if a general manager was too busy to have time to fill out the questionnaire, the questionnaire could be passed to other members of their top management team.

Fourth, considering the bias of the single informant approach, the research assistants were asked to try their best to get multiple informants from some of the samples, when they had the chance to interview other informants.

The final data collection was conducted in the six cities simultaneously in October 2008 to November 2008. A sample of 1100 enterprises was drawn from an enterprises database. 265 questionnaires were returned, of which 53 were incomplete and excluded from the sample, thus the effective response rate was 19.27%. Given the length of the questionnaire and the demand of the sample, the response rate is acceptable.

The *t*-test shows there is no significant difference between respondents and non respondents. Table 4. 1 presents an overview of the characteristics of the 212 firms studied and some descriptors of the organizations.

4.3 Measures

Previously validated scales were adopted for the survey

instrument. Although most items were from existing and extensively tested scales, I also refined the questionnaire and modified some items to adapt to Chinese context. Furthermore, all scales were subject to a series of reliability and validity assessments.

In this section, the measures of the dependent and independent variables in the model shown in Figure 1.1 will be presented. In this study, multiple-item measures were developed for all the constructs. Such scales are necessary to capture the domain of the constructs adequately and accurately (Churchill, 1979; Nunnally, 1978). This approach is believed to reduce measurement error and increase the reliability and validity of the measures (Churchill, 1979; Peter, 1979). All scales were subject to a series of reliability and validity assessments.

4.3.1 Measures of International Entrepreneurship

According to the definition of international entrepreneurship in Chapter 2, "International entrepreneurship is the discovery, enactment, evaluation, and exploitation of opportunities — across national borders — to create future goods and services". (Oviatt and McDougall, 2005 p. 540). McDougall and Oviatt (2000) also have applied the innovative, proactive and risking taking behavior to define international entrepreneurship. From the development of a definition, previous studies view international entrepreneurship as the sum of company's innovation, risk taking and proactiveness in internationalization. Following these efforts, these three dimensions were adopted for the construct of international entrepreneurship in this study. As known, the commonly used items were developed by Covin and Slevin (1989), Lumpkin and Dess (1996) and Smart and Conant (1994). I adopted the items from these studies. However, some items were modified.

These three dimensions of international entrepreneurship were measured using 7-point Likert scales ranging from 1 "to no extent" to 7 "to a great extent'. The respondents were asked to identify the collective management style of their business unit's key decision-maker rather than any one individual's management style or philosophy during their internationalization.

The measures of innovation were drawn from Covin and Slevin (1989), Lumpkin and Dess (1996) and Zhou (2007). Three items were used:

- Our top management always encourages new product ideas for international markets.
- Our top management is very receptive to innovative ways of

exploiting international market opportunities.

- Our top management believes the opportunity of international markets greater than that of domestic market.

The measures of proactiveness were drawn from Covin and Slevin (1989), Lumpkin and Dess (1996) and Zhou (2007). Four items were used:

- Our top managers have regularly attended local/ foreign trade fairs.
- Our top management actively seeks contact with suppliers or clients in international markets.
- Our top management regularly monitors the trend of export markets
- Our top management actively explores business opportunities abroad.

The measures of risk taking were drawn from Covin and Slevin (1989), Lumpkin and Dess (1996) and Zhou (2007). Three items were used:

- Our top management focuses more on opportunities than risks abroad.
- When confronted with decisions about exporting or other international operations, our top management is always tolerant to potential risks.

■ Our top management values risk-taking opportunities abroad.

4.3.2 Measures of Exploitative and Exploratory Learning

The exploitative and exploratory learning were measured using 7-point Likert scales ranging from 1 "to no extent" to 7 "to a great extent". The respondents were asked to indicate the extent to which their firms undertake significant effort in the described learning activities.

To measure exploitative learning, I adopted the six items from Gima and Murray (2006) and developed one new item that tapped the extent to which the learning activities focused on the acquisition of information and knowledge from existing sources for the purpose of internationalization.

The measures of exploitative learning were drawn from Gima and Murray (2006). Six items were used:

■ Exploiting current internal procedures regarding your international activities.

■ Exploiting current reward systems regarding your international activities

■ Exploiting current knowledge regarding local competitors

■ Exploiting current knowledge regarding local cooperative

agreements in your industry

- Exploiting current knowledge regarding local laws that affect your business
- Exploiting current knowledge regarding local business norms in your industry

Exploratory learning, measured by five items also from Gima and Murray (2006), tapped the extent to which learning activities were focused on searching for and using information for internationalization that was unrelated to the firm's current knowledge status for the purpose of experimentation.

The measures of exploratory learning were drawn from Gima and Murray (2006). Five items were used:

- Developing new internal procedures regarding your international activities
- Developing new reward systems regarding your international activities
- Developing new knowledge regarding local competitors
- Developing new knowledge regarding local cooperative agreements in your industry
- Developing new knowledge regarding local business norm in your industry

4.3.3 Measures of Internationalization of Organizational Field

In this study, the environment is conceptualized as an organizational field. With the internationalization of organizational field, the isomorphic pressure will force other firms to conform to go abroad. This isomorphic pull may come through coercive, mimetic, and normative pressures in their fields. The organizational field is the "totality of relevant actors" including those that may not actually interact directly. Consistent with the definition, firms see themselves in a global rather than local organizational field.

I measure the internationalization of organizational field with four items from Hessels and Terjesen (2008) to reflect the international extent in the home market in some specific industry.

- Domestic competitors increasingly operate abroad
- Domestic customers increasingly operate abroad
- Suppliers increasingly operate abroad
- Foreign competitors increasingly operate in home market

4.3.4 Measures of Performance

To measure performance, following the frequently used

approach to measure international performance in the extent literature, a relative, multidimensional and subjective measure was applied in this study. First, objective financial performances were unavailable for most of the sample because firms were reluctant to reveal their objective financial data as it was confidential. However, more complete performance information could be obtained using subjective measures (McDougall et al., 1994). Second, a narrow financial performance is often biased. Third, it has been indicated that managerial self-reportings have a strong correlation with internally objective performance measure (Dess and Robinson, 1984; Pearce, Robbins & Robinson 1987) and externally secondary published performance data (Venkatraman & Ramanujam 1986). Fourth, researchers have also argued that multiple performance measures should be used (McDougall et al., 1994; Prescott, 1986).

In this study, I attempted to measure a firm's performance along two dimensions: financial performance and market performance. I drew from an extensive literature search and interviews with managers. Finally, eight items on performance in foreign market were used in the questionnaire. Respondents were asked to compare their performance, covering a three-year period of exporting or other international activity, to the performance of their major competitor. All items were obtained on a seven-point scale, ranging from 1 to 7.

- Sales growth
- Pre-tax profitability
- Market share
- Development of image
- Return on investment abroad
- Return on sales abroad
- Sales abroad profitability
- As a whole

4.3.5 Control Variables

There are a number of variables that are believed to affect organizational performance. As noted by Murphy et al., (1996), failure to address these control issues may result in "biased relationship due to the possible noncomparability of firms in the sample" (p. 22). This study included several control variables that might affect the hypothesized relationships, including company age, company size, length of international experience and international scope. Company age was measured by the number of years a firm had been in existence. Company size was measured by the number of employees. International experience was measured by the number of years since the firm first began exporting/ being involved in international activity. International scope was the number of countries to which the firm exported its products.

4.4 Validity and Reliability of the Constructs

In order to test the research framework, a necessary requirement is to validate the constructs. As Peter (1981) indicated, "…such theories cannot develop unless there is a high degree of correspondence between abstract constructs and the procedures used to operationalize them" (p. 133).

Validity measures the extent to which a measure or set of measures correctly represents the concept of the study. Reliability refers to how it is measured. There are three commonly used validity criteria: content validity, convergent validity and discriminate validity. Reliability measures the extent to which a variable or set of variables is consistent in what it is intended to measure. Traditionally, the Cronbach's (1970) alpha is adopted to evaluate reliability. However, recently more studies use the confirmatory factor analysis to evaluate measurement scale (Hair et al. , 1998 ; Gerbing & Anderson, 1988). In this study, I used confirmatory factor analysis to test the reliability. In this section, both the validity and reliability were assessed because they provide necessary information for inferring construct validation (Bagozzi et al. , 1979; Churchill 1979; Peter 1981).

4.4.1 Content Validity

Content validity refers to the extent to which a measurement reflects a specific domain of content (Carmines & Zeller, 1979). Content validity in this study was addressed by reviewing the relevant literature to establish the domain of each construct. The items were adopted from existing and extensively tested scales. Moreover, the initial questionnaire was pretested. On the basis of pretesting, I modified the wordings of some items and developed the final instrument. Such procedures established content and face validity.

4.4.2 Convergent Validity

Construct validity refers to the extent to which the measure of a construct correctly measures the concept that it purports to measure (Cook & Campbell, 1979). There are two ways to assess construct validity: convergent validity and discriminate validity.

Convergent validity means that alternative measures of the same construct will relate strongly with one another (Carmines & Zeller, 1979). In this study, I tested the validity and reliability of the study's measurement models with confirmatory factor analysis (CFA) using AMOS 16.0. However, because of the restrictions of the sample size (Bentler & Chou, 1987; Doney & Cannon, 1997), I grouped theoretically related constructs to ensure acceptable estimate-to-observation ratios. The first CFA model (Model 1) included Organizational Filed, Proactivness, Innovativeness and Risk Taking. The second CFA model (Model 2) included Exploitative Learning, Exploratory Learning and Performance. The results indicated that both CFA models had acceptable fit (Model1: $\chi^2 = 102.14$, df = 57, χ^2/df = 1.79, goodness-of — fit [GFI] = 0.93, confirmatory fit index [CFI] = 0.97, root mean squared error of approximation [RMSEA] = .06; Model 2: $\chi^2 = 238.85$, df = 139, χ^2/df = 1.72, GFI = 0.90, CFI = 0.96, RMSEA = 0.06). Results of the CFA are presented in Table 4.2 and 4.3.

The results show that all items loaded significantly on their expected constructs. Moreover, significant cross-loadings were identified, supporting the convergent validity of the measurement items and the unidimensionality of the latent constructs. The overall fit of the model also indicated unidimensionality (Steenkamp & Van Trijp, 1991).

4.4.3 Discriminant Validity

Confirmatory factor analysis was also used for assessing discriminant validity. Discriminant validity means the measures of different construct have modest relationships with each other (Carmines & Zeller, 1979). In order to assess the discriminant validity, I followed the recommendation of Bagozzi and Phillips (1982) to conduct pairwise two-factor confirmatory analysis. For each pair of factors, I compared the $\chi 2$ values in a measurement model that constrained their correlation to 1 with a baseline measurement model without this constrain. The χ^2 difference tests performed for each pair of factors consistently revealed significant differences, which suggested all measures achieved discriminate validity. Results are presented in Table 4. 4. Therefore, all the measures achieved discriminant validity and all the dimensions in this study can be treated as distinct dimensions.

In summary, the internal consistency, convergent validity, and discriminate validity results indicated that the measurement model exhibited satisfactory properties. Therefore, the study proceeded to test the hypotheses.

4.4.4 Composite Reliability and Average Variance Extracted

To estimate the internal consistency of the constructs, the composite reliability (CR) and average variance extracted (AVE) were applied. Although the output of AMOS does not provide these two measures directly, the necessary information is offered.

The composite reliability of a construct is calculated as:

$$\text{Construct reliability (CR)} = \frac{(\Sigma \lambda_i)^2}{(\sum \lambda_i)^2 + \sum (1 - \lambda_i^2)}$$

The standard loadings are obtained from the AMOS output. According to the requirements, the CRs for all constructs were greater than the threshold of .7 (Hair et al., 1998).

The average variance extracted reflects the variance in the indicators accounted for by the latent construct. Higher AVE values indicate that the items are truly representative of the latent construct.

The average variance extracted is calculated as:

$$\text{Average Variance Extracted (AVE)} = \frac{\sum \lambda_i^2}{\sum \lambda_i^2 + \sum (1 - \lambda_i^2)}$$

Guidelines suggest that the AVE should be above the . 05 level (Hair et al. , 1998) which means that more than half of the variance observed was accounted for by the hypothesized constructs.

The CR and AVE for the major constructs in this study are reported in Table 4. 5. From the results, the AVEs risk taking and exploratory learning is below 0. 5. It is below the recommended 50 percent. Thus, in the future, special attention should be paid on these measurements. The scores of CR are all above 0. 7. In general, the results of AVEs and CRs indicate that the items in this study have met psychometric criteria for reliability and validity, and they are sufficient in their representations of the constructs.

4.5 Analysis Methods

4.5.1 Analysis Techniques

The research framework developed from Chapter 3 indicates two major underlying relationships among the constructs, one is the mediating effects of international entrepreneurship on organizational field and two kinds of learning, the other is that the inverted U-shape between two kinds of different leaning activities and performance.

I tested the hypotheses with hierarchical regression analyses on international entrepreneurship, exploitative learning, explorative learning and performance. Firstly, to test the mediation effect, I followed the regression procedures suggested by Baron and Kenny (1986).

To clarify the mechanism of mediating effect, Figure 4. 1 as a model for depicting a causal chain. From the diagram, it is a three-variable system: the direct impact of the independent variable (Pathc), the impact of mediator (Path b) and the path from the independent variable to the mediator (Path a).

To support the existence of the mediation effect, four conditions must be met (Baron & Kenny, 1986). That is, (1) the independent variable must affect the mediator; (2) the independent variable must affect the dependent variable; (3) the mediator must affect the dependent variable; (5). When path c is reduced to zero, there is strong evidence of a single, dominant mediator. If the residual Path c is not zero, this indicates the operation of multiple mediating factors. As Baron and Kenny (1986) mentioned because most areas of psychology have multiple causes, a more realistic goal is to seek mediators that significantly decrease Path c rather than eliminating the relation between the independent and dependent variables together. Therefore, a significant reduction demonstrates that the mediating effect exists.

Secondly, multiple regression analysis was adopted to test the inverted U-shape. According to the inverted U-shape relationship, the multiple regression analysis was applied. In order to test the inverted U-shape, the following equation should exist.

$$Y = aX^2 + bX + c \ (1).$$

In the equation (1), to support the existence of the inverted U-shape, the relationship between X^2 and Y should be significant. Moreover, the value of *a* should be negative.

4.5.2 Multicollinearity Problem

In this study, the hypotheses were tested using multiple regression analysis. Before taking the multiple regression analysis, multicollierarity should be diagnosed. Especially, I create squared terms in multiple regression analysis.

Multicollinearity refers to a problem with the presence of significant correlations among independent variables in regression model. The existence of multicollinearity tends to inflate the variances of predicted values and parameter estimates because the regression coefficients of any independent variable depend on other independent variables included in the model. The multicolliearity problem is more likely to occur when squared terms are included.

The widely used method for detecting the presence of multicollineartiy is by means of variance inflation factors (VIFs). These factors measure how much the variances of the estimated regression coefficients can be inflated as compared to when the independent variables are not linearly related. The VIF value is used as an indicator of the severity of multicolineartiy. When the value of VIF is over 10, the multicollinearity is considered as a serious problem and will influence the estimation (Neter et al., 1990). In order to resolve this problem, before creating the squared terms, the relevant variables were mean-centered (Crohbach, 1987).

4.5.3 Another Analysis Methods

As discussed above, confirmatory factor analysis was

conducted to assess the factor structure of organizational field, international entrepreneurship, exploratory learning, exploitative learning and performance. According to Hair et al., (1995), this method is useful in explaining these variables in terms of their common underlying dimensions or factors. According the CFA results, the reliability and validity of these constructs were checked.

In addition to the above mentioned methods, other analysis techniques were also adopted for different purposes. For example, *t*-test was used to compare the differences between the samples who respond at different times.

4.6 Chapter Summary

In this chapter, the methodological issues related to investigating the relationship among the internationalization of organizational field, international entrepreneurship, exploitative and exploratory learning and performance are discussed. The data of this study are from a sample of 212 international firms. The questionnaire was designed based on a comprehensive literature review and a pilot study. For data collection, the questionnaire based survey was adopted. The confirmatory factor analysis was used to assess reliability and validity of major constructs in the theoretical framework. The model was mainly tested by using multiple regression analysis.

Table 4.1 Descriptive Statistics for the 212 Sample Firms

Organizational Characteristics	Values	Numbers	Percentages
Size	Small Firms (no more than 100 employee)	29	13.68
	Medium Firms (more than 100 but less than 500 employees)	50	23.58
	Large Firms (more than 500 employees)	133	62.74
Years established	Six or less than six years	22	10.38
	More than six years	190	89.62
The year go abroad After establishment	*In ten year after establishment*	175	82.55
	Between 11 *to* 16 *years after establishment*	25	11.79
	Between 16 *to* 20 *years after establishment*	5	2.35
	More than 21 after establishment	7	3.30

Continued

Organizational Characteristics	Values	Numbers	Percentages
Ownership	State-owned Enterprises	22	10.38
	Private Enterprises	91	42.92
	Collective Owned Enterprises	10	4.72
	Foreign Invested Enterprises	25	11.79
	Others	64	30.19

Table 4.2 Models Fit Indexes

	Model1	Model 2
χ^2	102.14	238.85
df	57	139
χ^2/df	1.79	1.72
GFI	0.93	0.90
CFI	0.97	0.96
RMSEA	0.06	0.06

Table 4.3 Confirmatory Factor Analysis of Measures

Construct and Source	Operational Measures of Construct	SFL[a]	*t*-value
Model 1			
Organizational Field	1. Domestic competitors increasingly operate abroad.	.90	12.07
	2. Domestic customers increasingly operate abroad.	.68	9.68

Continued

Construct and Source	Operational Measures of Construct	SFL[a]	*t*-value
Organizational Field	3. suppliers increasingly operate abroad	.70	10.68
	4. Foreign competitors increasingly operate in home market	.88	11.91
Proactiveness	1. Our top management actively seeks contact with supplier or clients in international markets	.79	13.30
	2. Our top management regularly monitors the trend of export markets.	.90	16.06
	3. Our top management actively monitors the trend of export markets.	.83	14.16
	4. Our top management develops human and other resources for achieving our goals in international markets	.61	9.36
Innovativeness	1. Our top management always encourages new product ideas for international markets	.77	12.29
	2. Our top management is very receptive to innovative ways of exploiting international market opportunities.	.80	13.01
	3. Our top management believes the opportunity of international markets greater than that of domestic market.	.63	9.55

Continued

Construct and Source	Operational Measures of Construct	SFL[a]	t-value
Risk taking	1. Our top management focuses more on opportunities than risks abroad.	.60	8.11
	2. When confronted with decisions about exporting or other international operations, our top management is always tolerant to potential risks.	.77	10.34
	3. Our top management values risk-taking opportunities abroad.	.64	8.57
Model2	Model Fix Indexes: χ^2 = 238.85, df = 139, χ^2/df = 1.72, GFI = 0.90, CFI: 0.96, RMSEA: 0.06		
Exploitative Learning AVE = 0.51 CR = 0.86	1. Exploiting current internal procedures regarding your international activities	.66	10.31
	2. Exploiting current reward systems regarding your international activities	.71	11.35
	3. Exploiting current knowledge regarding local competitors	.64	9.91
	4. Exploiting current knowledge regarding local cooperative agreements in your industry	.69	10.91
	5. Exploiting current knowledge regarding local laws that affect your business	.82	13.74
	6. Exploiting current knowledge regarding local business norms in your industry	.75	12.39

Continued

Construct and Source	Operational Measures of Construct	SFL[a]	t-value
Exploratory Learning AVE = 0.48 CR = 0.82	1. Developing new internal procedures regarding your international activities	.67	10.23
	2. Developing new reward systems regarding your international activities	.71	11.17
	3. Developing new knowledge regarding local competitors	.67	10.44
	4. Developing new knowledge regarding local cooperative agreements in your industry	.77	12.37
	5. Developing new knowledge regarding local business norms in your industry	.66	9.95
Performance AVE = 0.58 CR = 0.92	1. Sales growth	.75	12.29
	2. pre-tax profitability	.76	12.55
	3. market share	.69	10.85
	4. development of image	.78	12.99
	5. Return on investment abroad	.85	14.84
	6. Return on Sales abroad	.72	11.57
	7. Sales abroad Profitability	.73	11.72
	8. as a whole	.78	13.06

[a] SFL = standardized factor loading. The scale format for each of these measures is 1 = "strongly disagree", and 7 = "strongly agree"

Table 4.4 Discriminant Validity

Model 1	Constrained Model	Unconstrained M-odel	χ^2 differnece and d. f
Proactiveness versus Innovative	χ^2 = 143.8 d. f. = 58	χ^2 = 102.1 d. f. = 57	χ^2 differnece = 41.7, d. f. = 1
Proactiveness versus Risk Taking	χ^2 = 201.8 d. f. = 58	χ^2 = 102.1 d. f. = 57	χ^2 difference = 99.7, d. f. = 1
Risk taking versus Innovative	χ^2 = 176.7 d. f. = 58	χ^2 = 102.1 d. f. = 57	χ^2 difference = 83.4, d. f. = 1
Innovative versus Institutional Environment	χ^2 = 167.5 d. f. = 58	χ^2 = 102.1 d. f. = 57	χ^2 difference = 65.4, d. f. = 1
Risk Taking versus Organization Field	χ^2 = 190.1 d. f. = 58	χ^2 = 102.1 d. f. = 57	χ^2 difference = 88, d. f. − 1
Exploitative Learning versus Exploratory Learning	χ^2 = 246.7 d. f. = 140	χ^2 = 238.9 d. f. = 238.9	χ^2 differnece = 7.2, d. f. = 1
Exploitative Learning and Performance	χ^2 = 497.2 d. f. = 140	χ^2 = 238.9 d. f. = 238.9	χ^2 differnece = 258.3, d. f. = 1
Exploratory Learning versus Performance	χ^2 = 351.5 d. f. = 140	χ^2 = 238.9 d. f. = 238.9	χ^2 difference = 112.6, d. f. = 1

Table 4. 5 Composite Reliability and Average Variance Extracted Estimates for Major Constructs

Construct	Average Variance Extracted	Composite Reliability
Organizational Field	0. 68	0. 86
Proactiveness	0. 62	0. 87
Innovativeness	0. 54	0. 80
Risk taking	0. 46	0. 71
Exploitative learning	0. 51	0. 86
Exploratory learning	0. 48	0. 82
Performance	0. 58	0. 92

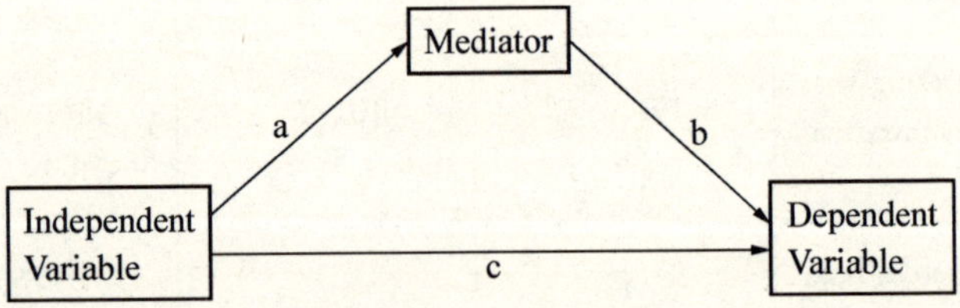

Figure 4. 1 The Mechanism of Mediating Effects

Chapter 5
Results and Hypotheses Testing

This chapter focuses on reporting the results of the tests of hypotheses presented in Chapter 3. This chapter includes the following sections. In the first section, the results concerning the main effects and the mediating effects are presented. The second section highlights the inverted U-shape of exploitative and exploratory learning on performance. And the last section is a summary of all of the findings.

5.1 Mean Scores and Correlation Coefficients

In testing the hypotheses, an index for each multiple-item scale was created. In this study, I followed the method provided by Nunnally (1978), summated score which is the simple aggregation and average of the raw item values were used to obtain the construct scores or index.

Table 5. 1 presents descriptive statistics and correlation coefficients of the constructs. Mean scores on the internationalization of organization field in Table 5. 1 indicate that, in general, firms face pressure from their environment. As anticipated, the mean score of international entrepreneurship is high. That indicates firms took entrepreneurial activities to acquire foreign opportunities. Regarding exploitative and exploratory learning, all international firms need to take learning activities to acquire foreign knowledge. Further analyses will be illustrated in the following study.

5.2 Tests of Direct Effect and Mediating Effects (H1 to H5)

5.2.1 Tests of Direct Effect (H1, H2 and H4)

As mentioned in the section of data analysis methods, the method of multivariate regression analysis is used to test the direct effect of the hypotheses.

The testing of hypotheses (H1, H2 and H4), multivariate regression analysis was conducted. I tested the effect of the internationalization of organizational field on international entrepreneurship and also tested the effects of international entrepreneurship on exploitative and exploratory learning.

The regression equations took the following forms.

Model 1:

International Entrepreneurship = $\beta_0 + \beta_1$Control Variables + β_2O. F. + Error

Model 2:

Exploitative Leaning = $\beta_0 + \beta_1$Control Variables + β_2I. E. + Error

Model 3:

Exploratory Leaning = $\beta_0 + \beta_1$Control Variables + β_2I. E. + Error

Where,

O. F. = the Internationalization of Organizational Field

I. E. = International Entrepreneurship

The results concerning the main effects are presented as standardized regression coefficients in Table 5.2. For model 1, the independent variable explained 31 percent of variance in international entrepreneurship (R^2 = 31%, Adjusted R^2 = 0.30, F value = 18.64). For model 2, the independent variable explained 36 percent of variance in exploitative learning (R^2 = 0.36, Adjusted R^2 = 0.35, F value = 23.18). For model 3, the independent variable explained 21 percent of variance in exploratory learning (R^2 = 0. 21, Adjusted R^2 = 0. 19, F value = 10. 79). Next, the results concerning each of the hypotheses (H1, H2 and H4) are presented.

H1, stating that the internationalization of organization field is positively related to international entrepreneurship, was supported. In model1, the results showed that regression coefficient of the internationalization of organizational field had a significantly positive relationship with international entrepreneurship (β = 0.53, p < 0.001). Thus H1 was supported.

H2 proposed that the international entrepreneurship is positively related to exploitative learning. The results showed that regression coefficients of international entrepreneurship had significantly positive relationship with exploitative learning (β = 0.60, p < .001). Thus H2 was supported.

H4 posited that international entrepreneurship is positively related to exploratory learning. As shown in Table 2, the regression coefficients of international entrepreneurship had significantly positive relationship with exploratory learning (β = 0.40, p < .001). Thus H4 was supported.

5.2.2 Tests of Mediating Effects (H3)

When testing hypotheses 3, which posits that international

entrepreneurship mediates the relationship between organizational field and exploitative learning, a series of multiple regression analyses were conducted following the instruction of Baron and Kenny (1986).

Model 1:

International Entrepreneurship = $\beta_0 + \beta_1$Control Variables + β_2O. F. + Error

Model 2:

Exploitative Leaning = $\beta_0 + \beta_1$Control Variables + β_2O. F. + Error

Model 3:

Exploitative Leaning = $\beta_0 +_{\beta 1}$Control Variables + β_2O. F. + β_3I. E. + Error

Where,

O. F. = the internationalization of Organizational Field

I. E. = International Entrepreneurship

The results of three regression analyses are presented as standardized regression in Table 5. 3. As indicated in Table5. 3, all the three models were significant. For Model 1, the independent variable explained 31 percent of variance in the international entrepreneurship (R^2 = 0. 31, Adjusted R^2 = 0. 30, F value = 18. 64). For Model 2, the independent variable explained 36 percent of variance in exploitative learning (R^2 =

0.36, Adjusted R^2 = 0.35 F value = 23.18). For Model 3, the independent variables explained 39 percent of variance in exploitative learning (R^2 = 0.39, Adjusted R^2 = 0.37 F value = 21.77). Model 1 indicated that the internationalization of organizational field had a positive ($\beta = .53$) and significant ($p < .001$) impact on international entrepreneurship. Model 2 revealed that the internationalization of organizational field had a positive ($\beta = 0.60$) and significant ($p < .001$) impacts on exploitative learning. When exploitative learning was regressed on organizational field and international entrepreneurship at the same time, in Model 3, the impact of organizational field on exploitative learning had been reduced ($\beta = 37$) and international entrepreneurship still had an positive ($\beta = 0.29$) and significant ($p < .001$) impact.

The results of the three regression models satisfied the four conditions of the existence of the mediating effect identified by Baron and Kenny (1986). The results of multiple regression analyses indicated that the internationalization of organizational field had an indirect impact on exploitative learning via international entrepreneurship. This is to say, international entrepreneurship mediates the relationship between the internationalization of organizational field and exploitative learning. The H3 is supported.

5.2.3 Tests of Mediating Effects (H5)

When testing hypotheses 5, which posits that international entrepreneurship mediates the relationship between organizational field and exploratory learning, a series of multiple regression analyses were conducted following the instruction of Baron and Kenny (1986).

Model 1:

International Entrepreneurship = $\beta_0 + \beta_1$Control Variables + β_2O. F. + Error

Model 2:

Exploratory Leaning = β_{0+} β_1Control Variables + β_2O. F. + Error

Model 3:

Exploratory Leaning = β_{0+} β_1Control Variables + β_2O. F. + β_3I. E. + Error

Where,

O. F = the Internationalization of Organizational Field

I. E = International Entrepreneurship

The results of three regression analyses are presented as standardized regression in Table 5.4. As indicated in Table5. 4, all the three models were significant. For Model 1, the independent variable explained 30 percent of variance in the international entrepreneurship (R^2 =0.30, Adjusted R^2 =0.31, F value =18.64). For Model 2, the independent variable explained 21 percent of variance in exploratory learning (R^2 =0. 21, Adjusted R^2 =0.19, F value =10.79). For Model 3, the independent variables explained 29 percent of variance in exploratory learning (R^2 =0.29, Adjusted R^2 =27, F value =14.62). Model 1 indicated that the internationalization of organizational field had a positive (β =0.53) and significant (p <001) impact on international entrepreneurship. Model 2 revealed that the internationalization of organizational field had a positive (β =0.40) and significant (p < 001) impacts on exploratory learning. When exploratory learning was regressed on organizational field and international entrepreneurship at the same time in Model 3, the impact of organizational field on exploratory learning had been non significant and international entrepreneurship still had a positive (β =0.35) and significant (p <001) impact.

The results of the three regression models satisfied the four conditions of the existence of mediating effect identified by Baron and Kenny (1986). The results of multiple regression analyses indicated that the internationalization of organizational field had an indirect impact on exploratory learning via international entrepreneurship. This is to say, international entrepreneurship mediates the relationship between organizational field and exploratory learning. The H5 is supported.

5.3 Tests of Invert U-shape (H6 and H7)

The testing of the hypotheses (H6 and H7) concerning the inverted U shape of exploitative and exploratory learning on performance was conducted by using multiple regression analyses. To remove the potential confounding effects of control variables, I include the variables of company age, company size, length of international experience and international scope as control variables.

Due to the square term in the equation, multicollinearity is especially a concern for analyzing Model3. As indicated in Chapter 4, prior to the creation of the square term, the independent variable were mean centered to reduce the potential problem of multicollinearity in suing regression analysis. I calculated the variance inflation factor (VIF) for each of the regression coefficient to assess the degree to which relations among the independent variables inflate the standard error. The VIF below 10 suggest that multicollinearity is unlikely to affect the parameter estimates (Neter, Wasserman & Kutner, 1990).

For testing the inverted U-shape, the following equations are used.

Model 1: Controls

Performance = $\beta_{0+}\beta_1$Age + β_2 Size$_+$ β_3Experience + β_4Scope + Error

Model 2: Controls + Main Effects + inverted U-shape

Performance = $\beta_{0+}\beta_1$Age + β_2 Size$_+$ β_3Experience + β_4Scope + β_5Exploitative Leaning + β_6Exploratory Leaning + β_7Square of Exploitative Learning + β_8 Square of Exploratory Learning + Error

The results concerning the control variable effects are presented as standardized regression in Table 5. 5. As indicated in Table 5. 5, all the two models were significant. For Model1, the independent variables explained 15 percent of variance in firm's performance (R^2 = 0. 15, Adjusted R^2 = 0. 13 F value = 9. 76). For Model 2, the independent variables explained 31 percent of variance in the firm's performance (R^2 = 0. 31, Adjusted R^2 = 0. 28, F value = 11. 27).

The model 3 provided support for hypotheses 6 and 7, which posits that the inverted U- shape between exploitative learning on performance, and exploratory learning on performance. The square of exploitative learning in the regression was negative (β = – 0. 18) and significant ($p < .01$) and the square of exploratory learning was negative (β = – 0. 12) and significant ($p < .10$). The explanatory power of this analysis (measured by the level of R square) is significant. The results in Model 2 indicated that the relationship between exploratory learning and performance and exploitative learning and performance are inverted U-shape. Therefore, the hypotheses 6 and 7 are supported.

5.4 Chapter Summary

This chapter reported the results of the hypotheses developed in Chapter 3. Descriptions were provided on the manner in which each of the hypotheses was tested. In summary, the results of this study indicate that: (1) the internationalization of organizational field is positively related with international entrepreneurship. (2) International entrepreneurship mediates the relationship between the internationalization of organizational field and exploitative and exploratory learning. (3) The relationship between exploitative learning and performance is an inverted U- shape. (4) The relationship between exploratory learning and performance is an inverted U-shape. A summary of the results for each of the hypotheses is provided in Table 5.6

The next chapter will discuss the results and implications, limitations and suggestions for further research.

Table 5.1 Descriptive Scores and Zero – Order Correlation Coefficients

	Mean	s. d.	1	2	3	4	5	6	7	8	9	10
1. Organizational Field	4093	1.07										
2. Proactiveness	5.30	1.19	0.44 *									
3. Innovativenss	4.75	1.08	0.42 *	0.59 *								
4. Risk taking	4.13	1.15	0.35 **	0.26 **	0.43 **							
5. Exploitative Learning	4.86	1.04	0.442 **	0.51 **	0.53 **	0.32 *						
6. Exploratory Learning	4.41	1.08	0.31 **	0.38 **	0.41 **	0.32 **	0.75 **					
7. Performance	4.14	0.86.	0.24 **	0.17 **	0.29 **	0.21 **	0.36 **	0.44 **				
8. Age	15.95	11.54	0.15 *	0.08	0.08	0.07	0.08	0.17 *	0.23 **			
9. Size	1958.0	3061.9	-0.81	0.03	0.11	0.02	0.12	0.12	0.12	0.00		
10. International Experience	9.30	6.09	-0.08	0.10	0.02	-0.03	0.03	0.10	0.20 **	0.63 **	0.00	
11. Country Number	8.63	11.26	0.25 **	0.19 **	0.25 *	0.14 *	0.17 *	0.21 **	0.21 **	0.32 **	0.06	0.25 **

Table 5.2 Results of Direct Effects

	Model1	Model2	Model3
	DV = IE	DV = Exploitative Learning	DV = Exploratory Learning
Independent Variables			
Organizational Field	.53 ***	.60 ***	.40 ***
IE			
Control Variables			
Firm Age	-.06	-.05	.07
Firm Size	.09	.12 *	.12 +
International Experience	.07	.05	.03
International Scope	.10	-.22	.05 **
R^2	.31	.36	.21
Adjusted R^2	.30	.35	.19
F Value	18.64 ***	23.18 ***	10.79 ***

Table 5.3 Results of Tests for Mediation by International Entrepreneurship

	H4: IE As a Mediator for Exploitative Learning		
	Model 1	Model 2	Model 3
	DV = IE	DV = Exploitative Learning	DV = Exploitative Learning
Independent Variables			

Continued

		H4: IE As a Mediator for Exploitative Learning	
	Model 1	Model 2	Model 3
Institutional Environment	.53***	.60***	.37*** ↓
IE			.29**
Control Variables			
Firm Age	-.06	-.05	-.02
Firm Size	.09	.12*	.10+
International Experience	.07	.05	.02
International Scope	.10	-.22	-.02
R^2	.31	.36	.39
Adjusted R^2	.30	.35	.37
F Value	18.64***	23.18***	21.77***

Note: Standardized regression coefficients are shown. + $p < .10$ * $p < .05$ ** $p < .01$ *** $p < .001$ DV = Dependent Variable; OE in HM = Organization Field. The symbol "↓" stands for a significant reduction in the estimated coefficient in Model 3 and Model 5 as compared with that in Model 2 and Model 4 respectively (It is the evidence for the mediation effect).

Table 5.4 Results of Tests for Mediation by International Entrepreneurship

		H5: IE As a Mediator for Exploratory Learning	
	Model 1	Model 2	Model 3
	DV = IE	DV = Exploratory Learning	DV = Exploratory Learning
Independent Variables			

Continued

		H5: IE As a Mediator for Exploratory Learning	
	Model 1	Model 2	Model 3
Institutional Environment	.53***	.40***	.11 ↓
IE			.35***
Control Variables			
Firm Age	-.06	.07	.11
Firm Size	.09	.12+	.09
International Experience	.07	.03	.00
International Scope	.10	.05**	.05
R^2	.31	.21	.29
Adjusted R^2	.30	.19	.27
F Value	18.64***	10.79***	14.62***

Note: Standardized regression coefficients are shown. $^+p<.10$ $^*p<.05$ $^{**}p<.01$ $^{***}p<.001$ DV = Dependent Variable; OE in HM = Organization Field. The symbol "↓" stands for a significant reduction in the estimated coefficient in Model 3 and Model 5 as compared with that in Model 2 and Model 4 respectively (It is the evidence for the mediation effect).

Table 5.5 Results of Tests for Inverted U-shaped Relationships

	Model 1 IV = Performance	Model 2 IV = Performance
Independent Variables		
Exploitative Learning		.07

Continued

	Model 1 IV = Performance	Model 2 IV = Performance
Explorative Learning		.27 **
Exploitative Learning Squared		–.18 *
Explorative Learning Squared		–.12 +
Control Variables		
Firm Age	.12	.09
Firm Size	.15 **	.08
International Experience	.03	.08
International Scope	.27 ***	.07
R^2	.15	.31
Adjusted R^2	.13	.28
F Value	9.76 ***	11.27 ***
$\triangle R^2$		.22
$\triangle F$		30.46 ***

Table 5.6 The Summary of the Results

Hypotheses	Support or Reject
H1: The internationalization of organizational field is the antecedent of international entrepreneurship.	Support
H2: International entrepreneurship is positively related to exploitative learning.	Support

Continued

Hypotheses	Support or Reject
H3: International entrepreneurship is positively related to exploratory learning.	Support
H4: International entrepreneurship mediates the relationship between the organizational field and exploitative learning.	Support
H5: International entrepreneurship mediates the relationship between organizational field and exploratory leaning.	Support
H6: Exploitative learning has an inverted U-shaped relationship with firm performance in foreign markets, such that the positive effect decreases after a threshold level.	Support
H7: Exploratory learning has an inverted U-shaped relationship with performance, such that the positive effect decreases after a threshold level.	Support

Chapter 6

Discussion, Implications, Limitations and Future Research

The final chapter discusses the empirical findings in Chapter 5. It aims to advance potential implications of the results in light of the research questions and theoretical models presented in Chapter 3. It also addresses the limitations of the current study and offers directions for further research.

This chapter is divided into six sections. First, the discussions of the results will be presented. Second, I will provide the contributions of the research. Third, research implication for theory development and managerial practices will be discussed. In the subsequent two sections, the limitations of the study and directions for future research are addressed. Finally, a brief summary of this study will be presented.

6.1 Discussion of Results

The following discussion is based on the results of the analyses presented in Table 5.6.

Results of the study indicated that: (1) the internationalization of organizational field is the antecedent of international entrepreneurship. (2) International entrepreneurship mediates the relationship between organizational field and exploitative learning. International entrepreneurship mediates the relationship between organizational field and exploratory learning. (3) Exploitative learning has an inverted U-shaped relationship with firm performance in foreign market. Exploratory learning has an inverted U-shaped relationship with performance. In the next section, I will discuss these results in detail.

The antecedent of international entrepreneurship

The findings of the study suggested that the internationalization of organizational field is the predicator of international entrepreneurship. As indicated previously, although the antecedent of international entrepreneurship has been widely investigated, few attempts have been made to investigate from the neoinstitutional perspective. Researchers have only concentrated on the organizational factors, firms' resources, and strategic factors to explain the possible antecedents of international entrepreneurship. However, not only the technical and organizational level factors, but also the institutional level factors may influence firms' behavior (Parsons, 1960; Petit, 1960).

Empirical results of this study showed that, after controlling for some control variables, the internationalization of organizational field is positively related with international entrepreneurship. The result is consistent with the hypotheses. Currently, with the globalization of the China market, such as the growth of foreign competitors, domestic competitors, suppliers and customers going abroad, some organizational fields becoming more and more international, the increasingly internationalization of the organizational fields provide firms with legitimacy to take international entrepreneurial activities.

The mediating effect of international entrepreneurship

The results show that international entrepreneurship mediate the relationship between organizational field and exploitative learning and the relationship between organizational field and exploratory learning. As known, the internationalization theory puts knowledge at the center of internationalization process. According to Eriksso et al., (1997), a lack of foreign market knowledge is a significant obstacle to a firm's internationalization. The knowledge regulates the resources committed to a foreign market (Eriksson et al., 1997). Moreover, it is a necessary driver in a firm's successful internationalization (Bikey and Tesar, 1978; Simmonds and Smith, 1968). After firms go abroad, firms will take some activities to get foreign knowledge. One possible reason is that, the legitimacy pressure from a host country dominates the firms' behaviors. Actually, besides the objective reason for achieving legitimacy, the subjective reason is that international entrepreneurial firms also provide the learning culture for acquiring host country knowledge.

One reason of the liability of foreignness arises from the lack of legitimacy in a host country (Zaheer, 1995). Host country specific knowledge is a driving force behind international expansion (Barkema & Vermeulen, 1997; Inkpen & Beamish, 1997). In order to get legitimacy and compete with local firms, firms have to be devoted to learning activities for acquiring host country specific knowledge which influences a firm's ability to adapt its products to local market conditions. Consistent with March's model, the organizational learning is classified into exploitative learning and exploratory learning. Furthermore, from the subjective perspective, international entrepreneurial firms also provide the learning culture for acquiring host country knowledge.

The result is consistent with the hypotheses. After firms go abroad, they take exploitative and exploratory learning activities to acquire foreign market knowledge.

The inverted-U shape of explorative and exploratory learning on performance

As I mentioned, the learning activities are classified as exploitative learning and exploratory learning. The results show that exploitative learning has an inverted U-shaped relationship with firm performance in foreign markets. That supports the hypotheses. The results also support the notion that exploratory learning has an inverted U-shape with firm performance in foreign markets.

Exploitative learning arises out of a necessity for firms to fully use their limited resources. This can reduce errors and avoid mistakes in internationalization (Eriksson et al., 2000). However, a high level of exploitation implies that a firm may lack the volume and diversity of new knowledge about host country that deviates substantially from current knowledge (Atuahene-Gima & Murray, 2007). Thus, excessive exploitation may lead to inefficiency and errors in a host country because of "familiarity traps" (Ahuja & Lampert, 2001) and organizational myopia (Audia, Locke & Smith, 2000; March, 1991).

During the process of internationalization, a firm also explores new knowledge beyond its existing capabilities and resources, which is exploratory learning. By providing new knowledge about a host country, exploration ensures that firms adapt to foreign environments and get legitimacy. Despite these advantages, there are high risks and costs associated with exploration. In addition, firms also should take time to understand and assimilate new knowledge. However, because of their absorptive capacity, firms do not fully understand the new knowledge. Even though they assimilate knowledge, limited resources may make firms fail in internationalization. Therefore, excessive exploration results in high costs from failed experiments and insufficient rewards from successful ones.

The result is consistent with the hypotheses. Although exploitation may make firm get legitimacy and enhance performance in foreign markets, beyond a certain point, it results in lower performance because of knowledge ossification.

Although exploration may be beneficial, after a certain point, it can diminish performance. Thus, exploratory learning has an inverted U-shaped relationship to performance, such that at low levels, its effect on performance is positive, but at a higher level, its effect on international performance tends to be negative.

6.2 Contributions

The purpose of this study is to contribute to the literature by integrating organizational field and organizational learning into international entrepreneurship study. This study investigated the internationalization of organizational field as the antecedent of international entrepreneurship from a neoinstitutional theory perspective. Incremental theory does not capture the phenomena of international new ventures and network theory does not explain a firm's internationalization without the help of network (Oviatt & McDougall, 1994). Extant research in international entrepreneurship explores the antecedent of international entrepreneurship from an organizational level and a firm level. However, the research has regarded the firm as a closed system and ignored the institutional environment level. The key theoretical insight here is that institutional isomorphism can reveal the antecedent of international entrepreneurship from a neoinstitutional perspective.

Second, the study also advances the literature on the consequence of international entrepreneurship. After firms go abroad, in order to conform to the norms of the local market to be accepted as legitimate entities, firms should get knowledge about a host country through learning activities. The theoretical insight here is that institutional isomorphism can reveal the consequences of international entrepreneurship from a neoinstitutional perspective.

Third, according to the learning theory, I divided the learning activities into exploitative and exploratory learning to investigate the relationship between learning and performance. This study also advances the literature on the non-liner relationship between two kinds of learning and performance.

Finally, this study was conducted in China. Few studies have been conducted on the related issues in non-U. S. settings as pointed out in Chapter1. China is an example of an emerging economy; the results could be generalizable to other countries.

This study offers the first investigation that applies neoinstitutional theory to explain the antecedents and consequences of international entrepreneurship. Thus, I offer a fresh model to describe the relationship between the internationalization of organizational field, international entrepreneurship, organizational learning and performance. In brief, by taking a first step toward understanding how institutional environment influence firms' international entrepreneurial activities, this study provides a road map.

6.3 Implications

This study has important implications for managers and policy makers. Firstly, to facilitate both exploitative and exploratory learning, managers should understand how the internationalization of organizational field affects firms to show international entrepreneurship and how international entrepreneurial firms survive in foreign markets. Furthermore, performance is affected by the level of the two types of learning. The inverted U-shaped relationships indicate that extreme levels of exploitative and exploratory learning are not beneficial to performance in foreign markets. In order to survive and prosper in foreign markets, managers should make a choice to maintain an appropriate level between exploitative and exploratory learning to improve performance.

Secondly, for Chinese policy makers, in order to stimulate firms to "go abroad", an effective means is to encourage foreign firms to come to China because the internationalization of organizational field will motivate Chinese firm to "go abroad". With the globalization of the world economy, more competitors, suppliers and customers will come into China and Chinese firms will go abroad. Chinese firms will face more pressures from the organizational field, which motivate them to engage in international activities. The "Open door" policies of the late 1970s and accession to WTO in 2001 are favorable policies to stimulate Chinese firms to go abroad.

6.4 Limitations and Directions for Future Research

There are a few limitations to this study that we should note. First, the questionnaire was developed from the extant literature. All original questions were in English. Even if the back-translation process is used, (Hoskisson, et al., 2000) translation problems can not be avoided. From the data analysis, the AVE values for risk taking and exploratory learning were under .5. According to the criteria, it is better that the AVE is above 0.5. Therefore, in further studies, the questionnaire should be modified, especially regarding these two variables.

The second limitation of the study was created by the data collection procedure. This study adopted availability sampling rather than the random sampling method (Keppel et al., 1992). Using this method, the top managers were invited to participate in the project on a voluntary basis. As a result, it was possible that the non-random sampling procedure may present some bias in the data. Thus, it is difficult to know how random or representative the sample is.

Third, this study relies mainly on the single key informant approach for data collection, which may cause a halo effect or common method variance. In further, using different sources of data for the independent and dependent variables would provide more robust evidence. Moreover, the data was only from top managers. So the study can not avoid the common method variance problem.

Fourth, the data was only collected from several cities of China. However, China is divided along several dimensions: the eastern and western provinces, high population density in the east and low density in the west, favored economic development plans for the east as opposed to the western provinces. Therefore, China's large area and the economic gap between the eastern and western region may limit the generalizability of the findings. In further studies, sample firms should also be drawn from other western regions in order to validate the findings of this study.

Fifth, the performance constructs used in the study were conceptualized as perceptual, as opposed to objective measure. Thus, it might have been biased by the relative optimism that the managers display (McCarthy, 1992). However, it would be difficult to gather objective performance in China. Therefore, in further, if financial and accounting data are made available, this limitation could be overcome.

Sixth, in this study, I only examined the exploitative and exploratory learning. However, they compete for firm's scarce resources, resulting in the need for firms to manage the tradeoffs between the two. Therefore, an appropriate balance between these two types of learning is a crucial factor in a firm's internationalization (March, 1991). In further study, I may extend the frame by balancing these two types of learning.

Finally, this study did not take into consideration relevant moderating variables, such as the environment in host countries. The environment in a host country might influence the exploitative or exploratory learning activities or their performance. Further research should incorporate relevant moderators to offer a more comprehensive explanation regarding these issues.

6.5 Conclusions

Incremental theory and network theory explain internationalization from different perspectives and have their own limitations (Mtigwe, 2006). Specifically, incremental theory does not capture the phenomena of international new ventures and network theory does not explain a firm's internationalization without the help of networks (Oviatt & McDougall, 1994). International entrepreneurship theory does not explain why a firm engages in entrepreneurial activities. The key theoretical insight here is that institutional isomorphism can reveal the antecedent of international entrepreneurship. In order to conform to the norms of the local market to be accepted as legitimate entities, firms should get knowledge about their host country through organization learning. The results also show the consequences of international entrepreneurship. In addition to these, the results of this study also advance the literature on their non-linear relationship to performance. The findings are that the relationship between exploitative learning, exploratory learning and performance has an inverted U-shape.

Extant research has confirmed that the institutional environment and organizational learning are critical to international entrepreneurship. However, few studies have examined the environment from a neoinstitutional theory perspective. In conclusion, this study specifies a rationale by which the institutional isomorphism drives firms to take international entrepreneurial activities and push them to take learning activities. Finally, the non-lincr rclationship bctwccn both cxploitativc and cxploratory learning and performance were examined.

References

Acedo, F. J. and Florin, J. (2006), An entrepreneurial cognition perspective on the internationalization of SMEs. *Journal of International Entrepreneurship*. 4(1),49 - 67.

Ahuja, G., and Lampert, C. M. (2001), Entreprenuership in the large corporation: A longitudinal study of how established firms create breakthrough inventions. *Strategic Management Journal*, 22(6/7),521 - 543.

Andersson, S. (2000), the Internationalization of the firm from an entrepreneurial perspective. *International Studies of Management and Organization*, 30(1),63 - 92.

Argote, L. (1999), *Organizational Learning: Creating, Retaining and Transferring Knoweldge*, Kluwer: Boston, MA.

Armagan, S., and Ferreira, M. P. (2005), The impact of political culture on firms' choice of exploitation-exploration:

internationalization strategy. *International Journal of Cross Cultural Management*, 5 (3) ,275 - 291.

Atuahene-Gima, K. , and Murray, J. Y. (2007), Exploratory and Exploitative Learning in New Product Development: A Social Capital Perspective on New Technology Ventures in China. *Journal of International Marketing*, 15(2) ,1 - 29.

Autio, E. , Sapienza, H. J. , and Almeida, J. G. (2000), Effects of age at entry, knowledge intensity, and limitability on international growth. *Academy of Management Journal*, 43(5) ,909 - 924.

Axelsson B. , and Easton, G. (eds.) (1992), Industrial networks: a new view of reality. Routledge, London.

Bagozzi, R. P. , and Phillips, L. W. (1982), Representing and testing organizational theories: A Holistic Construal, *Administrative Sciences Quarterly*, 27 (Septermber) ,459 - 489.

Bagozzi, R. P. , and Yi, Y. (1994), Advanced topics in structural equation models. in Bagozzi (eds) *Advanced Methods of Marketing Research*, Cambridge, Mass. : Blackwell Business: 1 - 51.

Bagozzi, R. P. , Tybout, A. M. , C. , Craig, S. and Sternthal, B. (1979), the Construct Validity of the Tripartite Classification of Attitudes. *Journal of Marketing Research*,

16 (February), 88 – 95.

Baird, I. S., and Thomas, H. (1985), Toward a contingency model of strategic risk taking. *Academy of Management Review*, 10, 230 – 243.

Barkema, H. G., and Vermeulen, F. (1997), What differences in the cultural backgrounds of partners are detrimental for international joint ventures? *Journal of International Business Studies*, 28(4), 845 – 864.

Baron, R. M., and Kenny, D. A. (1986), The moderator-mediator variable distinction in social psychological research: Conceptual, strategic, and statistical considerations. *Journal of Personality and Social Psychology*, 51(6), 1173 – 1182.

Barrett, N. J., and Wilkinson, I. F. (1986), Internationalisation behaviour, management characteristics of Australian manufacturing firms by level of international development. in Turnbull, P. W., Paliwoda, S. J. (Eds), *Research in International Marketing*, Croom Helm, Beckenham.

Bentler, P. M., and Chou, C. P. (1987), Practical issues in structural modeling. *Sociological Methods and Research*, 16 (August), 78 – 117.

Bilkey, W., and Tesar, G. (1977), the Export behavior of small sized Wisconsin manufacturing firms. *Journal of*

International Business Studies, 8,93 - 98.

Blomstermo, A., Eriksson, K., Lindstrand, A., and Sharma, D. D. (2004), The perceived usefulness of network experiential knowledge in the internationalizing firm. *journal of international management*, 355 - 373.

Bloodgood, J. M., Sapienza, H. J., and Almeida, J. G. (1996), the Internationalization of new high-potential U. S. ventures: Antecedents and outcomes. *Entrepreneurship Theory and Practice*, 20(4),61 - 78.

Brush, C. G. (1993), Factors motivating small companies to internationalize. *Entrepreneurship Theory and Practice*, 17 (3),83 - 86.

Buckley, P. J., Clegg, LJ., Cross, A. R., Liu, X., Voss, H., and Zheng, P. (2007), The Determinants of Chinese Outward Foreign Direct Investment. *Journal of International business studies*, 38,499 - 518.

Burgel, O., and Murray, G. C. (1998), The international activities of British start-up companies in high-technology industries: Differences between internationalisers and non-internationalisers. In P. D. Reynolds, W. D. Byrave, N. M. Carter, S. Manigart, C. M. Mason, G. M., and Shaver, K. (eds). *Frontiers of Entrepreneurship research*, Babson

Park, MA: Babson College, 447 – 463.

Burton, F. N., and Schlegelmilch, B. B (1987), Profile analysis of non-exporters versus exporters grouped by export involvement. *Management International Review*, 27(1), 38 – 49.

Busenitz, L. W., Gomez, C., and Spencer, J. W. (2000), country institutional profiles: unlocking entrepreneurial phenomena. *Academy of Management Journal*, 43, 994 – 1003.

Calantone, R. J., Schmidt, J. B., and Song, X. M. l (1996), Controllable Factors of New Product Success: A Cross-National Comparison. *Marketing Science*, 15(4), 341 – 358.

Camines, E. G., and Zeller, R. A. (1979), *Reliability and Validity Assessment*, Beverly Hills: Sage Publication Inc.

Cavusgil, S. T. (1984), Differences Among Exporting Firms Based on Their Degree of Internationalization. *Journal of Business Research*, 12(2), 195 – 208.

Cavusgil, S. T. (1980), On the Internationalization Process of Firms. *European Research* 8, 273 – 281.

Chetty, S., and Holm, D. B. (2000), Internationalisation of small to medium-sized manufacturing firms: a network approach. *International business review*, 9(1), 77 – 93.

Chetty, S., and Campbell-Hunt, C. (2003), Explosive

international growth and problems of success amongst small to medium-sized firms. *International Small Business Journal*, 21(1),5 – 29.

Child, J., and Rodrigues, S. B. (2005), The Internationalization of Chinese Firms: A case for Theoretical Extension. *Management and Organization Review*, 1,381 – 410.

Churchill, G. A. (1979), A Paradigm for Developing Better Measures of Marketing Constructs. *Journal of Marketing Research*, 16(February),64 – 73.

Cohen, W. M., and Levinthal, D. A. (1990), Absorptive Capacity: A New Perspective On Learning And Innovation. *Administrative Science Quarterly*, 35(1),128 – 154.

Collins, R. (1979), the Credential Society. New York: Academic Press.

Cook, T. D., and Campbell, D. T. (1979), *Quasi-Experimentation: Design and Analysis Issues for Field Settings.* Chicago: Rand McNally.

Coviello, N., and Munro, H. (1997), Network relationships and the internationalisation process of small software firms. *International business review*, 361 – 386.

Coviello, N. E., and McAuley, A. (1999), Internationalisation and the smaller firm: A review of contemporary empirical *research. Management International Review*. Wiesbaden: Third Quarter 39(3),223 – 256.

Coviello, N. E., and Munro, H. J. (1995), Growing the entrepreneurial firm: Networking for international market development. *European Journal of Marketing*, 29(7),49 – 61.

Covin J. G., and Slevin D. P. (1989), Strategic management of small firms in hostile and benign environments. *Strategic Management Journal*. 10(1),75 – 87.

Covin, J. G., and Slevin, D. P. (1991), A conceptual model of entrepreneurship as firm behavior. *entrepreneurship: theory and practice*, 16(1),7 – 25.

Craig, C. S., and Douglas, S. P. (1996), Developing strategies for global markets: An evolutionary perspective. *Columbia Journal of World Business*, 31(1),70 – 81.

Cronbach, L., (1970), *Essentials of Psychological Testing*, 3rd edition. Harper & Row Publishers, Inc., New York.

Cronbach, L. J. (1987), Statistical Tests for Moderator Variables: Flaws in Analyses Recently Proposed. *Psychological Bulletin*, 102(3),414 – 417.

Cyert, R. M., and March, J. G. (1963), a *Behavioral Theory of the Firm* Englewood Cliffs, N. J.: Prentice-Hall, Inc.

Denis, J., and Depelteau, D., (1985), Market knowledge

diversification and export expansion. *Journal of International Business Studies*, 16 - 77.

Dess, G. G., Ireland, R. D., Zahra S. A., Floyd, S. W., Janney, J. J. and Lane, P. J. (2003), Emerging Issues in corporate entrepreneurship. *Journal of Management*, 29(3), 351 - 378.

Dess, G. G., Lumpkin, G. T., and Covin, J. G. (1997), Entrepreneurial strategy making and firm performance: Tests of contingency and configurational models. *Strategic Management Journal*, 18(9), 677 - 695.

Dess, G. G. and Robinson, R. B. Jr. (1984), Measuring Organizational performance in the Absence of Objective Measures. *Strategic Management Journal*, 5(3), 265 - 273.

Dhanaraj, C. and Beamish, P. W. (2003), A resource-based approach to the study of export performance. *Journal of Small Business Management*, 41(3). 242 - 261.

Dichtl, E.., Leibold, M., Koglmayr, H. G. and Muller, S., (1984), The Export Decision of Small and Medium-sized Firms: a Review. *Management International Review*, 24 (2), 49 - 60.

DiMaggio, P. and Powell, W. (1983), The iron cage revisited: Institutional isomorphism and collective rationality in organizational fields. *American Sociological Review*, 48 (2), 147 - 160.

DiMaggio, P. J. (1983), State expansion and organizational fields. In R. H. Hall & R. E. Quinn (Eds.), *Organizational theory and public policy*: 147 - 161. Beverly Hills, CA: Sage.

Dimitratos, P. and Jones, M. (2005), Future directions for international entrepreneurship research. *International business Review*, 14, 119 - 128.

Doney, P. M., Cannon, J. P. (1997), an Examination of the nature of trust in buyer-seller relationships. *Journal of Marketing*. 61(2), 35 - 51.

Dunning, J. H. (2006), Comment on Dragon Multinationals: New players in 21st century Globalization. *Asia Pacific Journal of Management*, 23, 139 - 141.

Ellis, P. (2000), Social ties and foreign market entry. *Journal of International Business Studies*, 31(3), 443 - 469.

Ellis, P. and Pecotich, A. (2001), Social factors influencing export initiation in small and medium-sized enterprises. *Journal of Marketing Research*. 38(1), 119 - 130.

Eriksson, K., Johanson, J., Majkgard, A. and Sharma, D. D. (1997), Experiential knowledge and cost in the internationalization process. *Journal of International Business Studies*, 28(2),337 - 362.

Eriksson, K., Johanson, J., Majkgard, A., and Sharma, D. D. (2000), Effect of variation on knowledge accumulation in the internationalization process. *International Studies of Management & Organization*, 30(1),26 - 44.

Eriksson, K., Johanson, J., Majkgard, A., and Sharma, D. D. (1997), Experiential knowledge and cost in the internationalization process. *Journal of International Business Studies*, 28(2),337 - 362.

Floyd, S. W. and Lane, P. J. (2000), Strategizing throughout the organization: Management role conflict in strategic renewal. *Academy of Management*. The Academy of Management Review. 25(1),154 - 177.

Fontes, M. and Coombs, R. (1997), The coincidence of technology and market objectives in the internationalization of new technology-based firms. *International Small Business Journal*, 15(4),14 - 35.

Forsgren, M. (1989), *Managing the internationalization process — The Swedish case*. New York: Routledge.

Garvin, D. A. (1993), Building a learning organization. *Harvard Business Review*, 71(4),78 - 91.

Gasses, Y. (1982), Elaborations on the psychology of the entrepreneur. In C., A. Kent, D. L. Sexton, and K. H. Vesper, eds., *Encyclopedia of Entrepreneurship*, Englewood Cliffs, NJ: Prentice-Hall, 57 - 71.

George, G. and Prabhu, G. N. (2000), Developmental financial institutions as catalysts of entrepreneurship in emerging economies. *The Academy of Management Review*, 25(3), 620 - 629.

Gerbing, D. W. and Anderson, J. C. (1988), An updated paradigm for scale development incorporating unidimensionality and its assessment. *Journal of Marketing Research*, 25 (May), 186 - 92.

Hair, J. F. Jr., Anderson, R. E., Tatham, R. L. and Black, W. C. (1998), *Multivariate Data Analysis*, Fifth Edition, Prentice Hall.

Hedlund, G. and Kverneland, A., (1985), Are strategies for foreign markets changing?. In: The case of Swedish investment in Japan, *International Studies of Management and Organization*, 15, 41 - 59.

Hisrich, R. D., Honig-Haftel, S., McDougall, P. P. and Oviatt B. M. (1996), Guest editorial: International entrepreneurship: Past, present, and future. *Entrepreneurship*

Theory and Practice, 20(4),5 - 10.

Hitt, M. A. and Bartkus B. (1997), International entrepreneurship. In J. Katz (ed.), *Advances in entrepreneurship, firm emergence and growth*: 3: 7 - 30. Greeenwich, CT: JAI Press.

Hook, R. K. and Czinkota, M. R. (1988), Export activities and prospects of Hawaiian firms. *International Marketing Review*, 5(4),51 - 57.

Hoskisson, R. E., Eden, L., Lau, C. M. and Wright, M. (2000), Strategy in emerging economies. *Academy of Management Journal*, 43(3),249 - 267.

Huber G. P. (1991), Organizational learning: the contributing processes and the literature. *Organization Science*, 2(1),88 - 115.

Inkpen, A. C. and Beamish, P. W. (1997), Knowledge, bargaining power, and the instability of international joint ventures. *The Academy of Management Review*. 22(1),177 - 202.

Javagli, R. G, Lawson, D., Gross A. C. and White, D. S (1998), Firm characteristics and export propensity: a comparison of manufacturers and manufacturing-based service providers. *International Business Review* 7(5),521 - 534.

Johanson J. and Mattson L. G. (1988), Internationalization in industrial systems: A network approach. In: Hood N, Vahlne J-E(eds), *Strategic in global competition*: 287 - 314. Croom Helm, London.

Johanson J. and Wiedersheim-Paul F. (1975), The internationalization of the firm: Four Swedish case studies. *Journal of management studies*, 12,305 - 322.

Johanson, J. and Vahlne, Jan-Erik (2003), Business relationship learning and commitment in the internationalization process. *Journal of International Entrepreneurship*, 1 (1), 83 -101.

Johanson, J. and Vahlne, Jan-Erik (1977), the Internationalization process of the firm — A model of knowledge development and increasing foreign market commitments. *Journal of International Business Studies* (pre - 1986). 8(1),23 - 32.

Johanson, J., and Vahlne, Jan-Erik. (1990), The Mechanism of Internationalisation

International Marketing Review, 7(4)11 - 24.

Johanson. J., and Vahlne, J. E., (1992), Management of foreign market entry, *International Business Review*, 1(3),9 - 27.

Johansson, J. K. and Nonaka, I. (1983), Japanese Export Management. *International Marketing Review*, 1, 2 (Winter), 12 - 25.

Jolanda H. and Terjesen, S. A. (2008), SME Direct and Indirect Export Modes: Resource Dependency & Institutional Theory Perspectives. *the proceeding of Academy of Management*, CA.

Jones, M. V. and Coviello, N. E. (2005), Internationalisation: conceptualising an entrepreneurial process of behaviour in time. *Journal of International Business Studies*. 36(3), 284 - 303.

Karafakioglu, M. (1986), Export activities of Turkish manufacturers. *International Marketing Review*, 34 - 43.

Karagozoglu, N. and Lindell, M. (1998), Internationalization of small and medium-sized technology-based firms: An exploratory study. *Journal of Small Business Management*, 36(1), 44 - 59.

Keiser, S. and Sproul, L. (1982), Managerial responses to changing environments: Perspectives on problem sensing from social cognition. *Administrative Science Quarterly*, 27(4), 548 - 570.

Keppel, G., Saufley, W. H. Jr. and Tokunaga, H. (1992), *Introduction to Design and Analysis*, 2nd ed. New York: W. H. Freeman and Company.

Khandwalla, P. N. (1977), *The design of organizations*. New

York: Harcourt Brace Jovanovich.

Kitchell, S. (1995), Corporate culture, environmental adaptation, and innovation adoption: a qualitative/quantitative approach. *Journal of the Academy of Marketing Science*, 23(3), 195-205.

Klaus E. M., and Nguyen, H. V. (2005), Foreign Investment Strategies and Sub-national Institutions in Emerging Markets: Evidence from Vietnam. *The Journal of Management Studies*, 42(1), 63-95.

Knight, G. (2000), Entrepreneurship and marketing strategy: The SME under globalization. *Journal of International Marketing*. 8(2), 12-32.

Knight, G. A. and Cavusgil, S. T. (2004), Innovation, organizational capabilities, and the born-global firm. *Journal of International Business Studies*, 35(4), 334-353.

Kreiser, P. M., Marino, L. D. and Weaver, K. M. (2002), Assessing the psychometric properties of entrepreneurial orientation scale: A Multi-Country Analysis. *Entrepreneurship: Theory and Practice*, 71-94.

Kuivalainen, O., Sundqvist, S. and Servais, P. (2007), Firms' degree of born-globalness, international entrepreneurial orientation and export performance, *Journal of World Bus-*

iness, 42(3),253 - 267.

Kuivalainen, O., Sundqvist, S., Puumalainen, K. and Cadogan, J. W (2004), The effect of environmental turbulence and leader characteristics on international performance: are knowledge-based firms different?, *Journal of Administrative Sciences*, 21(1),35 - 50.

Larson, M. S. (1977), *The rise of professionalism: A sociological analysis.* Berkeley: University of Califor-nia Press.

Levinthal, D. A. and March, J. G. (1993) The myopia of learning. *Strategic Management Journal*, 14,95 - 114.

Liesch, P. W. and Knight, G. A. (1999), Information internalization and Hurdle Rates in small and medium enterprise internationalization. *Journal of International Business Studies*, 30(2),383 - 394.

Loane, S. and Bell, J. (2006), Rapid internationalisation among entrepreneurial firms in Australia, Canada, Ireland and New Zealand. *International Marketing Review*, 23(5),467 - 485.

Lumpkin, G. T. and Dess, G. G. (1996), Clarifying the entrepreneurial orientation construct and linking it to performance. *The Academy of Management Review*, 21(1),135 - 172.

Lumpkin, G. T. and Dess, G. G. (2001), Linking two dimensions of entrepreneurial orientation to firm performance: The moderating role of environment and industry life cycle. *Journal of Business Venturing*, 16(5),429-453.

Lyles, M. A. and Schwenk, C. R. (1992), Top management, strategy and organizational knowledge structures. *Journal of Management Studies*, 29(2),155-174.

Madhok, A. (1996), Know-how-, experience-and competition-related considerations in foreign market entry: an exploratory investigation. *International Business Review*, 5(4),339-66.

Madhok, A. (1997), Cost, value and foreign market entry mode: The transaction and the firm. *Strategic Management Journal*, 18(1),39-61.

Madsen, T. K. and Servais, P. (1997), The internationalization of born globals: An evolutionary process? *International Business Review*, 6(6),561-583.

March, J. G. (1991), Exploration and Exploitation in Organizational Learning. *Organization Science*, 2(1),71-87.

Matsuno, K., Mentzer, J T. and Ozsomer, A. (2002), the Effects of Entrepreneurial Proclivity and Market Orientation on Business Performance. *Journal of Marketing*. 66(3),18-32.

McDougall, P. P. (1989), International versus domestic entrepreneurship: new venture strategic behavior and industry structure. *Journal of Business Venturing*, 4(6),387 – 400.

McDougall, P. P. and Oviatt, B. M. (1996), New venture internationalization, strategic change, and performance: A follow-up study. *Journal of business venturing*, 11(1),23 – 40.

McDougall, P. P., Shane, S. and Oviatt, B. M. (1994), Explaining the formation of international new ventures: The limits of theories from international business research. *Journal of Business Venturing*. 9(6),469 – 487.

McDougall, P. P. (1989), International versus domestic entreprcncurship: ncw vcnturc stratcgic bchavior and industry structure. *Journal of Business Venturing*. 4(6),387 – 500.

McDougall, P. P. and Oviatt, B. M. (1996), New venture internationalization, strategic change, and performance: A follow-up study. *Journal of business venturing*, 11(1),23 – 40.

McDougall, P. P. and Oviatt, B. M. (2000), International entrepreneurship: The intersection of two research paths. *Academy of Management Journal*, 43(5),902 – 908.

McDougall, P. P., Covin, J. G., Robinson, Jr., R. B. and Herron, L. (1994), The Effects of Industry Growth and Strategic Breadth on New Venture Performance and Strategy Content. *Strategic Management Journal*, 15(7),537 – 554.

McDougall, P. P., Shane, S. and Oviatt, B. M. (1994), Explaining the formation of international new ventures: The limits of theories from international business research, *Journal of Business Venturing*. 9(6),469-487.

McDougall, P. P. and Oviatt, B. M. (1997), International entrepreneurship literature in the 1990s and directions for future research. In D. L. Sexton & R. W. Smilor (Eds), *Entrepreneurship* 2000 (pp. 291-320). Chicago: Upstart Publishing.

McDougall, P. P. and Oviatt, B. M (2000), International entrepreneurship: The intersection of two research paths. *Academy of Management Journal*. 43(5),902-909.

Meyer, J. W. and Scott, W. R (1983), Centralization and the legitimacy problems of local government. In J. W. Meyer & W. R Scott (Eds.), *Organizational Environments: Ritual and rationality*: 199-215.

Meyer, J. W. and Rowan, B. (1977), Institutionalized Organizations: Formal Structure as Myth and Ceremony. *The American Journal of Sociology*, 83(2),340-363.

Miller, D. (1983), the correlates of entrepreneurship in three types of firms, *Management Sciences*, 29(7),770-791.

Miller, D. and Friesen, P. H. (1978), Archetypes of strategy formulation. *Management Science*, 24, 921-933.

Miller, D. and Friesen, P. H. (1980), Innovation in Conservative and Entrepreneurial Firms: Two Models of Strategic Momentum. *Strategic Management Journal*, 3(1),1-26.

Mittelstaedt, J. D., Ward, W. A. and Nowlin, E. (2006), Location, industrial concentration and the propensity of small US firms to export; Entrepreneurship in the international marketplace. *International Marketing Review*. 23(5),486-503.

Mizruchi, M. S. and Fein, L. C. (1999), The social construction of organizational knowledge: A study of the uses of coercive, mimetic, and normative isomorphism. *Administrative Science Quarterly*, 44(4),653-683.

Moen, O., Gavlen, M. and Endresen, I. (2004), Internationalization of small, computer software firms: entry forms and market selection. *European Journal of Marketing*, 38(9/10) 1236-1247.

Morris, M. H. and Sexton, D. L. (1996), the Concept of entrepreneurial intensity: implications for company performance. *Journal of Business Research*, 36, 5-13.

Morris, M. H., and Paul, G. W. (1987), The relationship between entrepreneurship and marketing in established firms. *Journal of Business Venturing*. 2(3),247-259.

Morrow, J. F. (1988), International entrepreneurship: A new

growth opportunity. *New Management*, 3, 59 - 61.

Mort, G. S. and Aerawardena, J. (2006), Networking capability and international entrepreneurship; How networks function in Australian born global firms.

International Marketing Review, 23(5),549 - 552.

Mtigwe, B. (2006), Theoretical milestones in international business: The journey to international entrepreneurship theory. *Journal of International Entrepreneurship*, 4(1),5 - 27.

Murphy, G. D., Jeff W. T. and Hill, R. C. (1996), Measuring Performance in Entrepreneurship Research. *Journal of Business Research*, 36(1),15 - 23.

Naman, J. L. and Slevin, D. P. (1993), Entrepreneurship and the concept of fit: A model and empirical tests. *Strategic Management Journal*. 14,137 - 153.

Neter, J., Wasserman, W. and Kutner, M. H. (1990), *Applied Linear Statistical Models: Regression, Analysis of Variance, and Experimental Designs*, 3rd ed. Homewood, IL: Richard D. Irwin, Inc.

Nunnally, J. C. (1978), *Psychometric Theory*, 2nd edition. McGraw-Hill Book Company, New York.

Oviatt, B, M. and McDougall, P. P. (1994), Toward a theory of international new ventures. *Journal of International Busi-*

ness Studies, 25(1),45 - 66.

Oviatt, B. M. and McDougall, P. P. (1995), Global start-ups: Entrepreneurs on a worldwide stage. *The Academy of Management Executive*, 9(2),30 - 45.

Oviatt, B. M. and McDougall, P. P. (2005), The internationalization of entrepreneurship. *Journal of International Business Studies.* Washington: 36(1),2 - 9.

Oviatt, B. M. and McDougall, P. P. (2005), Defining international entrepreneurship and modeling the speed of internationalization. *Entrepreneurship Theory and Practice*, 29(5),537 - 553.

Oviatt, B. M. and McDougall, P. P. (1994), Toward a Theory of International new ventures. *Journal of International Business Studies*, 25(1),45 - 44.

Oviatt, B. M. and McDougall, P. P. (1995), Global start-ups: Entrepreneurs on a worldwide stage. *The Academy of Management Executive*, 9(2),30 - 45.

Oviatt, B. M. and McDougall, P. P. (2005), The internationalization of entrepreneurship. *Journal of International Business Studies*, 36(1),2 - 9.

Parsons, T. (1960), *Structure and Process in Modern Societies* (New York: the Free Press of Glencoe, Chapters 1, 2.

Pearce, J. A. , Robbins, D. and Robinson, R. B. (1987), The Impact of Grand Strategy and Planning Formality on Financial Performance. *Strategic Management Journal*, 8(2),125 - 134.

Peng, M. W. and Heath, P. S. (1996), The growth of the firm in planned economies in transition: Institutions, organizations, and strategic choice. *Academy of Management Review*, 21, 492 - 528.

Penrose, E. (1959), *the Theory of the Growth of the Firm*, New York: Wiley.

Peter, J. P. (1981), Construct Validity: A Review of Basic Issues and Marketing Practices. *Journal of Marketing Research*, 18 (May), 133 - 145.

Petit, T. A. (1967), A Behavioral Theory of Management A Behavioral Theory of Management. *The Academy of Management Journal*, 10(4),341 - 350.

Powell, W. W. and DiMaggio, P. J. (1991), *The New institutionalism in organizational Analysis.* Chicago: University of Chicago Press.

Powell, W. W. and DiMaggio, P. J. (1991), *The new institutionalism in Organization Analysisi.* Chicago: University of Chicago Press.

Prescott, J. E. (1986), Environments as Moderators of the Relationship Between Strategy and Performance. *Academy of Management Journal*, 29(2),329 – 346.

Quinn (Eds.), *Organizational theory and public policy*: 147 – 161. Beverly Hills, CA: Sage

Racela, O. C., Chaikittisilpa, C. and Thoumrungroje, A. (2007), Market orientation, international business relationships and perceived export performance. *International Marketing Review*, 24(2),144 – 163.

Reter, J. P. (1979), Reliability: A Review of Psychometric Basics and Recent Marketing Practices. *Journal of Marketing Research*, 16(February),6 – 17.

Reuber, A. R. and Fischer, E. (1997), The influence of the management team's international experience on the internationalization behaviors of SMEs. *Journal of International Business Studies*,28(4),807 – 825.

Samiee, S. and Walters, P. G. P. (1990), Influence of firm size on export planning and performance. *Journal of Business Research*, 20(3),235 – 248.

Sapienza, H. J., Clercq, D. D. and Sandberg, W. R. (2005), Antecedents of international and domestic learning effort. *Journal of Business Venturing*. 20(4)437 – 457.

Schumpeter, J. (1934), *the Theory of Economic Development.*

Cambridge, Mass. : Harvard University Press.

Scott, W. R (1987), the Adolescence of institutional theory. *Administrative Science Quarterly*, 32, 493 – 511.

Scott, W. R. (1995), *Institutions and organizations*, Thousand Oaks: Sage Publications

Shane, S. and Venkataraman, S. (2000), the Promise of entrepreneurship as a field of research. *Academy of management review*, 25(1), 217 – 226.

Sharma, D. D. and Blomstermo, A. (2003), The internationalization process of Born Globals: a network view. *International Business Review*, 12, 739 – 753.

Sharma, S., Durand, R. M. and Gur-Arie, O. (1981), Identification and analysis of moderator variables. *Journal of Marketing Research*, 18 (August), 291 – 300.

Shaw, V. and Darroch, J. (2004), Barriers to Internationalization: A study of entrepreneurial new ventures in New Zealand. *Journal of International Entrepreneurship.* 2(4), 327 – 344.

Shrader, R. C., Oviatt, B. M. and McDougall, P. P. (2000), How new ventures exploit trade-offs among international risk factors: Lessons for the accelerated internationization of the 21st century. *Academy of Management Journal*, 3(6), 1227 – 1247.

Simmonds, K. and H. Smith, (1968), The first export order: A marketing innovation, *British Journal of Marketing* 2(2), 93 – 100.

Smart, D. T. and Conant, J. S. (1994), Entrepreneurial orientation, distinctive marketing competencies and organizational performance. *Journal of Applied Business Research*, 10(3), 18 – 28.

Spender J-C, Grant RM. (1996), Knowledge and the firm: overview. *Strategic Management Journal*, Winter Special Issue 17, 5 – 9.

Steenkamp, J. B. E. M. and van Trijp, H. C. M. (1991), The use of LISREL in validating marketing constructs. *International Journal of Research in Marketing*, 8, 349 – 377.

Steensma, K., Marino, L., Weaver, M. and Dickson, P. (2000), The influence of national culture in the formation of technology alliances by entrepreneurial firms. *Academy of Management Journal*, 43(5), 951 – 973.

Stevenson, H. H. and Gumpert, D. G. (1985), the Heart of entrepreneurship. *Harvard Business Review*, 85(2), 85 – 95.

Stevenson, H. H. and Jarillo, J. C. (1990), A paradigm of entrepreneurship: entrepreneurial management. *Strategic Management Journal*, 11, 17 – 27.

Sullivan, D. and Bauerschmidt, A. (1990), Incremental Internationalization: A Test of Johanson and Vahlne's Thesis. *Management International Review*, 30(1), 48-64.

Thoumrungroje, A. and Tansuhaj, P. (2005), Entrepreneurial Strategic Posture, International Diversification, and Firm Performance. *Multinational Business Review*, 13(1), 55-37.

Timmons, J. A. (1978), Characteristics and role demands of entrepreneurship. American

Journal of Small Business, 3, 5-17.

Tolbert, P. S. and Zucker, L. G. (1983), Institutional sources of change in the formal structure of organizations: The diffusion of civil service reform, 1880-1935. *Administrative Science Quarterly*, 28(1), 22-39.

Tompson, J. D. (1967), *Organizations in Action.* New York: McGraw-Hill.

Toyne, B. (1989), International exchange: A foundation for theory building in international business. *Journal of International Business Studies*, 20(1), 1-17.

Venkatraman, N. and Ramanujam, V. (1986), Measurement of Business Performance in Strategy Research: A Comparison of Approaches. *Academy of Management Review*, 11(4), 801-814.

Verwaal, E. and Donkers, B. (2002), Firm size and export intensity: solving an empirical puzzle. *Journal of International Business Studies*, 33(3):603-613.

Welch, C. L. and Welch, L. S. (2004), Broadening the concept of international entrepreneurship: internationalisation, networks and politics. *Journal of International Entrepreneurship*, 2(3) 217-237.

Welch, L. and Luostarinen, R. (1988), Internationalization — evolution of a concept. *Journal of General Management*, 14 (2), 34-55.

Westhead, P., Wright, M. and Ucbasaran, D. (1998), The internationalization of new and small firms. In P. D. Reynolds, W. D. Byrave, N. M. Carter, S. Manigart, C. M. Mason, G. D. Meyer and K. G. Shaver (eds), *Frontiers of entrepreneurship research*: 464-77. Babson Park, MA: Babson College.

Wilkinson, T. J. and Brouthers, L. E. (2000), Trade Shows, Trade Missions and State Governments: Increasing FDI and High-Tech Exports. *Journal of International Business Studies*. 31(4), 725-734.

Wright, M., Filatotchev, I., Hoskisson, R. E. and Peng, M. W. (2005), Strategic research in emerging economies: Challenging the conventional wisdom. *Journal of Management*

Studies, 42(1),1 – 33.

Wright, R. W. and Ricks, D. A. (1994), Trends in international business research: Twenty-five years. *Journal of International Business Studies*, 25(4),687 – 701.

Yang, Y. S., Leone R. P. and Alden, D. L (1992), A market expansion ability approach to identify potential exporters. *Journal of Marketing*, 56,84 – 96.

Yiu, D. W., Lau, ChungMing and Bruton, G. D (2007), International Venturing by Emerging Economy Firms: the Effects of Firm Capabilities, Home Country Networks, and Corporate Entrepreneurship. *Journal of International Business Studies.* 38(4),519 – 540.

Yli-Renko, H., Autio, E. and Tontti, V. (2002), Social capital, knowledge, and the international growth of technology-based new firms. *International business review*, 279 – 304.

Young, S., Hamill, J., Wheeler, C. and Davies, J. R. (1989), *International Market Entry and Development*, Hemel Hempstead: Harvester Wheatsheaf.

Zaheer, S. (1995), Overcoming the liability of foreignness. *Academy of Management Journal*, 38(2),341 – 363.

Zahra S. A., Jennings, D. F. and Kuratko, D. F. (1999), The Antecedents and consequences of firm-level entrepreneurship:

The state of the field. *Entrepreneurship: Theory and Practice*, 24(2),45－66.

Zahra, S. A, Ireland, R. D. and Hitt, M. A. (2000), International expansion by new venture firms: International diversity, mode of market entry, technological learning, and performance. *Academy of Management Journal*, 43(5),925－950.

Zahra, S. A. (1993), Conceptual model of entrepreneurship as firm behavior: a critique and extension. *Entrepreneurship theory and practice*, 14(4),5－21.

Zahra, S. A. and George, G. (2002), International entrepreneurship: the current status of the field and future research agenda, strategic entrepreneurship. *Blackwell Publishers Ltd.* 255－288.

Zahra, S. A. and Garvis, D. M. (2000.), International corporate entrepreneurship and firm performance: The moderating effect of international environmental hostility.
Journal of Business Venturing, 15(6),469－492.

Zahra, S. A. and Bogner, W. C. (1999), Technology strategy and software new ventures' performance: Exploring the moderating effect on the competitive environment. *Journal of Business Venturing*, 15,135－173.

Zahra, S. A., Neubaum, D. O, and Huse, M. (1997), the

Effect of the environment on export performance among telecommunications new ventures. *Entrepreneurship Theory and Practice*, 22(1),25－46.

Zhou, Lianxi (2007), the Effects of entrepreneurial proclivity and foreign market knowledge on early internationalization. *Journal of World Business*, 42(3),281－295.

Appendix 1

Chinese Version of Questionnaire

Thank you for your agreeing to complete the questionnaire. Your time and cooperation in completing it much appreciated. All questions should be answered based on the actual situations in your firm. There is no right or wrong answers to the questions. Please skip any questions if you can not remember the answer. All the data will be only used in academic study and your confidentiality will be guaranteed.

Part A: International Entrepreneurship

The following statements are meant to identify the collective management style of your business unit's key decision-makers rather than any one individual's management style or philosophy in your firm's internationalization. Please indicate by circling the appropriate number the extent to which the following statements characterize the management style of your business unit's top manager.

1. In general, the top managers of my firm favor⋯.

Proactiveness

	Strongly Disagree			Difficult to say			Strongly Agree
a. Our top management actively seeks contact with suppliers or clients in international markets.	1	2	3	4	5	6	7
c. Our tope management regularly monitors the trend of export markets	1	2	3	4	5	6	7
c. Our top management actively explores business opportunities abroad	1	2	3	4	5	6	7
d. Our top management develops human and other resources for achieving our goals in international markets	1	2	3	4	5	6	7

Innovativeness

	Strongly Disagree			Difficult to say			Strongly Agree
a. Our top management always encourages new product ideas for international markets.	1	2	3	4	5	6	7

b. Our top management is very receptive to innovative ways of exploiting international market opportunities.	1	2	3	4	5	6	7
c. Our top management believes the opportunity of international markets greater than that of the domestic market.	1	2	3	4	5	6	7

Risk taking

	Strongly Disagree			Difficult to say			Strongly Agree
a. Our top management focuses more on opportunities than risks abroad.	1	2	3	4	5	6	7
b. When confronted with decisions about exporting or other international operations, our top management is always tolerant to potential risks.	1	2	3	4	5	6	7
c. Our top management values risk-taking opportunities abroad.	1	2	3	4	5	6	7

Part B: International learning effect

Please indicate the extent to which your firm undertakes significant effort in:

Exploitative Learning

	Strongly Disagree			Difficult to say			Strongly Agree
a. Exploiting current internal procedures regarding your international activities	1	2	3	4	5	6	7
b. Exploiting current reward systems regarding your international activities	1	2	3	4	5	6	7
c. Exploiting current knowledge regarding local competitors	1	2	3	4	5	6	7
d. Exploiting current knowledge regarding local co operative agreements in your industry	1	2	3	4	5	6	7
e. Exploiting current knowledge regarding local laws that affect your business	1	2	3	4	5	6	7
f. Exploiting current knowledge regarding local business norms in your industry	1	2	3	4	5	6	7

Exploratory Learning

	Strongly Disagree			Difficult to say			Strongly Agree
a. Developing new internal procedures regarding your international activities	1	2	3	4	5	6	7
b. Developing new reward systems regarding your international activities	1	2	3	4	5	6	7

c. Developing new knowledge regarding local competitors.	1	2	3	4	5	6	7
d. Developing new knowledge regarding local cooperative agreements in your industry	1	2	3	4	5	6	7
e. Developing new knowledge regarding local business norms in your industry	1	2	3	4	5	6	7

Part C: Organization field

Please indicate the internationalization extent of your firm's environment.

Organization field

	Strongly Disagree			Difficult to say			Strongly Agree
a. Domestic competitors increasingly operate abroad	1	2	3	4	5	6	7
b. Domestic customers increasingly operate abroad	1	2	3	4	5	6	7
c. Domestic suppliers increasingly operate abroad	1	2	3	4	5	6	7
d. Foreign competitors increasingly operate in home market	1	2	3	4	5	6	7

Part D Performance

On average, how would you compare the performance of your company to that of your major competitors in the last three years?

Performance

	Strongly Disagree			Difficult to say			Strongly Agree
a. Sales growth	1	2	3	4	5	6	7
b. pre-tax profitability	1	2	3	4	5	6	7
c. market share	1	2	3	4	5	6	7
d. development of image	1	2	3	4	5	6	7
e. Return on investment abroad	1	2	3	4	5	6	7
f. Sales abroad Profitability	1	2	3	4	5	6	7
g. As a whole	1	2	3	4	5	6	7

Part E: Company Background

1. Company Name: ____________________
2. When was your firm established? ____________________
3. When did your firms go abroad ____________________
4. Number of Employees: ____________________
5. Major Products/Services: ____________________
6. How many counties did your firms export the products to ____________________

7. Does your firm have overseas sales? Yes/ No

If yes, how many percentages of your total sales are from overseas? ______________

8. Please tick in the right box of the appropriate ownership type:

(1) State Owned Enterprise □

(2) Collective Owned Enterprise: □

(3) Private Enterprise: □

(4) Foreign-owned Enterprise: □

(5) Others: (Please specify ___________________)

Appendix 2

Chinese Version of Questionnaire

企业调查问卷

第一部分:公司创业精神

以下是关于贵公司进入国外市场及在国外市场经营过程中,高层管理者的管理风格或理念的描述。请您在最贴切描述的数字上画勾:

1. 开拓性:总的来说,我们公司高层管理者	非常不同意	比较不同意	有点不同意	既不同意,也不反对	有点同意	比较同意	非常同意
(1) 主动与国外市场上的供应商或客户联系	1	2	3	4	5	6	7

续 表

(2) 经常关注出口市场的发展趋势	1	2	3	4	5	6	7
(3) 主动寻找国外市场的商机	1	2	3	4	5	6	7
(4) 为开拓和发展国外市场,专门配置所需要的资源	1	2	3	4	5	6	7
2. 创新性:总的来说,我们公司高层管理者							
(1) 一直鼓励为国外市场开发新产品	1	2	3	4	5	6	7
(2) 愿意采纳开拓国外市场的创新方法	1	2	3	4	5	6	7
(3) 相信国外市场的机会多于国内	1	2	3	4	5	6	7
3. 冒险性:总的来说,我们公司高层管理者							
(1) 关注国外的机会多于关注风险	1	2	3	4	5	6	7

续 表

(2) 当面对国际经营决策(比如出口)时,愿意接受潜在的风险	1	2	3	4	5	6	7
(3) 特别重视国外有风险的商业机会	1	2	3	4	5	6	7

第二部分:组织学习

以下是关于贵公司进入国外市场以及国际经营过程中组织学习行为的描述,请您在能最贴切描述贵公司在下列行为中努力程度的数字上划勾(1 表示非常不努力,7 表示非常努力,越接近 1,则表明公司越不努力,越接近 7,则代表越努力):

利用式学习:总的来说,我们公司	非常不努力	比较不努力	有点不努力	一般	有点努力	比较努力	非常努力
(1) 利用目前存在的企业国际经营的内部程序	1	2	3	4	5	6	7
(2) 利用目前存在的企业国际经营的报酬系统	1	2	3	4	5	6	7
(3) 利用目前存在的当地竞争对手的信息	1	2	3	4	5	6	7

续 表

(4) 利用目前存在的行业内的合作机会	1	2	3	4	5	6	7
(5) 利用目前存在的有关当地国际经营的法律知识	1	2	3	4	5	6	7
(6) 利用目前存在的有关当地商业经营规范的知识	1	2	3	4	5	6	7
探索式学习:总的来说,我们公司							
(1) 创建新的企业国际经营的内部程序	1	2	3	4	5	6	7
(2) 建立新的企业国际经营报酬系统	1	2	3	4	5	6	7
(3) 探索新的当地竞争对手的信息	1	2	3	4	5	6	7
(4) 探索新的行业内合作机会	1	2	3	4	5	6	7
(6) 探索新的有关当地商业经营规范的知识	1	2	3	4	5	6	7

第三部分 企业经营的国内与国外环境。以下是有关国内外环境特征的描述,请您在最贴切的描述数字上画勾:

1. 国内环境:目前国内市场中,我们所在行业	非常不同意	比较不同意	有点不同意	既不同意也不反对	有点同意	比较同意	非常同意
(1)行业内越来越多国内竞争者进入国外市场	1	2	3	4	5	6	7
(2) 行业内越来越多国内客户进入国外市场	1	2	3	4	5	6	7
(3) 行业内越来越多国内供应商进入国外市场	1	2	3	4	5	6	7
(4) 行业内越来越多国外竞争者进入中国市场	1	2	3	4	5	6	7

第四部分:企业绩效

1. 平均而言,近三年贵公司的绩效与行业内的主要竞争对手相比如何?

	低很多	低一些	低一点	差不多	高一点	高一些	高很多
(1) 国外销售额增长	1	2	3	4	5	6	7
(2) 国外销售收益率	1	2	3	4	5	6	7

续 表

	低很多	低一些	低一点	差不多	高一点	高一些	高很多
(3) 国外投资回报	1	2	3	4	5	6	7
(4) 国外销售回报	1	2	3	4	5	6	7
(5) 国外市场份额	1	2	3	4	5	6	7
(6) 国外销售税前利润	1	2	3	4	5	6	7
(7) 国外形象的树立	1	2	3	4	5	6	7
(8) 整体上	1	2	3	4	5	6	7

第五部分公司背景

1. 公司名称：________________________

2. 贵公司哪一年成立：________

3. 公司员工数量：________ ________

4. 贵公司所属行业类型：(请在行业类型方框处划勾)：

制造业□	运输业□	服务业□	农业□	批发商业□	零售商业□
其他(列出)______________					

5. 贵公司哪一年产品开始销售到国外市场：________________

6. 贵公司在成立多久后产品开始销售到国外市场：(请在以下时间范围内划勾)

成立后 6 年内□	成立后 7 - 10 年内□	成立后 11 - 16 年内□	成立后 16 - 20 年内□	成立后 21 年以上□

7. 请您在贵公司的公司所有制形式方框后面划对勾。

(1) 国有企业□

(2) 民营企业□

(3) 集体企业□

(4) 合资企业□

(5)外商独资企业□

(6) 其他 :(请详述________________)

图书在版编目(CIP)数据

国际企业家精神与合法化:基于中国国际企业的研究/杨海儒著.—上海:上海三联书店,2015.8
ISBN 978-7-5426-5228-7

Ⅰ.①国… Ⅱ.①杨… Ⅲ.①跨国公司-企业管理-研究-中国 Ⅳ.①F279.247

中国版本图书馆CIP数据核字(2015)第148772号

国际企业家精神与合法化——基于中国国际企业的研究

著　　者/杨海儒

责任编辑/冯　静
装帧设计/汪要军
监　　制/李　敏
责任校对/张大伟

出版发行/上海三联书店
(201199)中国上海市都市路4855号2座10楼
网　　址/www.sjpc1932.com
邮购电话/24175971
印　　刷/上海叶大印务发展有限公司

版　　次/2015年8月第1版
印　　次/2015年8月第1次印刷
开　　本/890×1240　1/32
字　　数/220千字
印　　张/6.375
书　　号/ISBN 978-7-5426-5228-7/F·714
定　　价/36.00元

敬启读者,如发现本书有印装质量问题,请与印刷厂联系021-66019858